Wild Shrubs

Wild Shrubs

Finding and Growing Your Own

by Joy Spurr

Pacific Search Press

Pacific Search Press, 715 Harrison Street, Seattle, Washington 98109
© 1978 by Joy Spurr. All rights reserved
Printed in the United States of America

Edited by Betsy Rupp Fulwiler
Designed by Paula Schlosser
Illustrated by Sally Dickman
Photography by Joy Spurr

Cover: Salal (*Gaultheria shallon*) flower

Library of Congress Cataloging in Publication Data
Spurr, Joy.
    Wild shrubs: finding and growing your own.
    Bibliography: p.
    Includes index.
    1. Flowering shrubs—Northwest, Pacific. 2. Shrubs—Northwest, Pacific.
3. Wild flower gardening—Northwest, Pacific. I. Title.
SB435.52.N6S67   635.9'76'09795   78-805
ISBN 0-914718-29-0

Contents

Metric and English Measurements **6**
Preface **7**
Introduction **11**
Propagation **15**
Plant Names and Identification **23**
Forty Wild Shrubs **27**
Landscaping Guide **84**
Nurseries and Public Collections **86**
Authors' Names Used in Botanical Designations **87**
Glossary **89**
Further Reading **92**
Index **93**

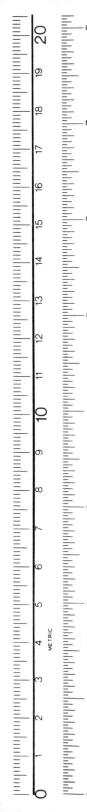

Metric and English Measurements

Botanists throughout the world use the metric system for all measurements. The plant identification information in this book, therefore, is given in the metric form. However, *Wild Shrubs* is also designed for those who are not yet familiar with the metric system, so all general information outside the botanical identification areas is presented in the English form.

The following chart indicates the relationship between the two systems. The ruler will help you use either system in the field when you are identifying native wild shrubs.

1 millimetre (1 mm) = 0.039 inches or 1/25 of an inch
1 centimetre (1 cm) = 0.393 inches or 2/5 of an inch
1 decimetre (1 dm) = 3.937 inches
1 metre (1 m) = 39.37 inches = 3.28 feet = 1.09 yards

10 mm = 1 cm
10 cm = 1 dm
10 dm = 1 m

Preface

Wild Shrubs is for anyone who enjoys plants. It is planned to aid amateur gardeners who have no special facilities for plant propagation but who may want to blend into their home landscape some of the flowering, wild shrubs. The descriptions, illustrated by photographs and drawings, provide accurate botanical information that will aid gardeners, naturalists, and all outdoor enthusiasts to identify the native shrubs they see in their travels around the countryside. Through this book, it is my desire to share with you my knowledge, experience, and deep appreciation of the utility and charm of the handsome wild shrubs that grow in the Pacific Northwest.

Acknowledgments

I am gratefully indebted to friends who have given freely of advice and guidance that has enabled me to propagate native shrubs and acquire, over a period of many years, the knowledge and experience that is shared in *Wild Shrubs:* Brian O. Mulligan, Director 1947-1973, Joseph A. Witt, Curator of Plants, and Richard van Klaveren, Plant Propagator, at the University of Washington Arboretum; Dr. Daniel E. Stuntz, mycologist and botanist; Dr. Leo Hitchcock, botanist; John W. Thompson, botanist; and The Arboretum Foundation. I also want to thank those at Pacific Search Press who made the production of *Wild Shrubs* possible: Harriet Bullitt, Alice Seed, Jane Lister Reis, Paula Schlosser, Judy Petry, and Betsy Rupp Fulwiler.

Introduction

Every section of the United States is well endowed with a broad spectrum of native shrubs that grow in a specialized habitat and are found nowhere else in the world in their native state. The Pacific Northwest is no exception. Its wild shrubs have survived many centuries of testing; their presence is proof of their ability to tolerate diseases, pests, and the most extreme growing conditions of their habitat. With a little effort and patience on your part, many species of wild shrubs can become choice garden ornamentals because they adapt easily to conditions in the home landscape and need only minimum care once they are established. The variety of shapes and sizes, intriguing blossoms, showy fruits, and interesting textures of foliage and bark challenge the gardener to use these hardy plants in interesting combinations with nursery-grown exotics.

During the early nineteenth century, European botanists came to the northwest coast in sailing ships, and were excited by the beauty of the native shrubs. They took many specimens of live plants and seeds to their home countries, where they grew and propagated them in botanical gardens. Today many native northwest plants are prized ornamentals in European and Asian gardens.

Botanists and plant enthusiasts still travel many miles to view the incredibly beautiful northwest shrubs. During May and June, the state flower of Washington—western rhododendron (*Rhododendron macrophyllum*)—puts on a magnificent display of pink flowers and awes the many viewers who travel far to see it in its few limited habitats (mainly Washington's Olympic Peninsula and the slopes and foothills of Oregon's Mount Hood). The beauty and fragrance of western azalea (*Rhododendron occidentale*) attracts flower lovers to the southern Oregon coast. Ancient geologic upheavals left remnants of this plant isolated in mountain valleys, so it also grows now in only a few scattered areas. Hikers wander into mountain country where trails are bordered with mountain box (*Pachistima myrsinites*) and white heath (*Cassiope mertensiana*). East-siders travel to the west side of the Cascade Mountains in late fall to pick the fruits of evergreen huckleberry (*Vaccinium ovatum*) or venture into coastal bogs for a glimpse of white-flowering Labrador tea (*Ledum groenlandicum*). West-siders travel the same routes to view mock orange (*Philadelphus lewisii*) or to collect the fruits of serviceberry (*Amelanchier alnifolia*), both hardy shrubs that survive hot, dry summers and freezing winters on the eastern slopes of the Cascades.

You can have these handsome shrubs in your own backyard by propagating the plants (by cuttings, seeds, layering, or stolons) or by buying the plants from nurseries (see "Nurseries and Public Collections"). You will then not only experience the thrill of achievement, but will also provide your garden with beautiful, interesting sights throughout the year.

In order to save time and effort when planning a garden, you first should formulate a landscape plan. To create a pleasant, functional, and personal environment, you need to know how the special characteristics of each plant can be used to the best advantage. Study the form, line, and texture value of each plant and decide how they can be combined with other plants and materials, including paths, walls, fences, and your house. Consider the growing habit of each shrub. Is it spreading or upright? What is its matured height and width? The invasive qualities of each plant must also be considered. (Shrubs are generally thought to be stationary, but some shrubs *walk* to increase their species.) Knowledge of a plant's creeping habit will suggest where and how it may best be used. For example, if you need to cover a large area of ground or if you want a grouping of plants, using the drifting habit of some plants in your plan can result in a natural design that grows rapidly.

Many native shrubs may grow in your immediate vicinity but have been overlooked because of their familiarity. If wild shrubs are already growing in your yard, give them the merit they deserve by designing them into your garden scheme. Salal (*Gaultheria shallon*) and low Oregon grape (*Berberis nervosa*), for instance, are common evergreen shrubs that produce colorful flowers and furnish edible fruits for the birds and for you.

What purpose plants are to serve in your garden is another important consideration. Fruit, leaves, and branching patterns are important when you want shrubs to blot out unpleasant views, serve as windbreaks, or form hedges that define property lines and areas within the garden. If you plant shrubs near the house, choose kinds that will not soon outgrow their locations. In areas where water conservation is a concern, plants that resist drought have a distinct advantage in the garden. Even in areas of adequate rainfall, choosing plants that have minimum water needs can reduce both maintenance and maintenance costs. The smaller the garden, the more important it is to have shrubs arranged in a pattern that is complementary throughout the year. Flowers may be on display only two or three weeks in a season so, to have year-round color, you will want to choose shrubs that bloom at different times.

Soil, moisture, drainage, light, and exposure conditions in your garden must also be studied before you make your final plant selection. By observing wild shrubs in their natural growing conditions, you can learn a lot about their needs. For example, evergreen huckleberry (*Vaccinium ovatum*) and mountain box (*Pachistima myrsinites*) usually grow in filtered shade beneath conifer trees. Sweet gale (*Myrica gale*), Labrador tea (*Ledum groenlandicum*), and bog laurel (*Kalmia polifolia*) grow in thickets and, as they are always in need of a continuous supply of water at their feet, grow in swamps or beside streams and lakes. At the same time, they need open sky above them so they can receive full benefit of the sun's rays throughout the day.

The low growing kinnikinnick (*Arctostaphylos uva-ursi*) and sticky laurel (*Ceanothus velutinus*) like good drainage. Both plants have a shrubby habit and thick leaves, adaptations that conserve moisture for the shrubs over a long period of time. This allows them to survive in hot, exposed areas where there is little rainfall and the soil is dry much of the summer.

Exposure to endless days of fog and salt spray in the coastal regions is not agreeable to most inland desert plants, but shrubs such as red currant (*Ribes sanguineum*) and ocean spray (*Holodiscus discolor*) thrive in many different kinds of habitats and seem to be equally happy in either moderate elevations inland or in seaside locales. The Oregon grapes (*Berberis aquifolium* and *B. nervosa*) are utilized for roadside plantings and in landscape plans for industrial buildings because they can withstand polluted air and automobile fumes.

When planning your garden, also give serious thought to including shrubs that attract, feed, and shelter birds. At a time when birds are losing more and more nesting areas and are threatened by pesticides, this is becoming increasingly important. Birds like a choice of places for their activities—from the tops of tall shrubs to low ground covers—and a variety of foods—seeds, fruits, flowers, and buds. Birds that choose your garden as a sanctuary will reward you with song and beauty, and their daily activities will be a never-ending source of pleasure.

In a natural garden, a balance of nature exists that allows flora to be healthy—free of pests and diseases—without your using pesticides that are dangerous to wildlife and humans. Birds, for instance, are an important part of nature's balance and care for your plants by eating insects. An occasional insect-blemished leaf is a small price to pay for keeping the garden free of chemicals and safe for you, birds, and other wildlife.

In acquiring the shrubs you choose for your garden, you must be aware of the rules for collecting wild shrubs. Because plant nurseries seldom stock a wide variety of shrubs that grow wild in their immediate vicinity, you may collect these shrubs by making ground layerings or by taking cuttings or seeds from public or private land. Also, you may sometimes dig plants, with permission from the landowners, on property that is scheduled for changes by highway construction, housing projects, or agriculture. Keep in mind, however, that *it is unlawful to collect plant material on public or private land without first obtaining permission from the proper authorities or the landowner.* When you receive permission to collect, conform to the owner's regulations so that others coming later will gain the same privilege.

Propagation

Although large shrubs are difficult to transplant from the wild, there are other ways to bring them into your garden. Shrubs can be propagated *asexually* (by vegetative parts) and *sexually* (by seeds). These methods do not injure the plant or mar the environment, and during the growth interval, you experience a sense of achievement when the plant parts root (or the seeds germinate) and develop into mature, healthy specimens.

Cuttings

Asexual or vegetative propagation is accomplished by means of cuttings, divisions, or layers. The new plant contains the same genetic material as its parent and so is identical to it. Cuttings offer the best way to propagate many of the wild shrubs. Pieces of stems are cut from the shrub and inserted in a rooting medium of clean, coarse sand; vermiculite; or a mixture of sand and peat or sand and perlite.

Propagation by cuttings is especially practical if you need many plants for a mass planting in a special area or for a ground cover. Those who feel they cannot afford to buy several dozen plants or think distance makes collecting in the wild impractical can purchase one or more plants from a nursery that specializes in native shrubs, and propagate cuttings from these plants (see "Nurseries and Public Collections").

It is impossible to give an exact date for taking cuttings of each species of shrub because the variable elevations and climatic conditions in which each plant grows affect the ripening of the wood. As a general rule, a plant is ready for cuttings if the wood breaks with a snap when bent. If it merely crushes between the fingers, it is too young; if it bends without breaking, it is too old. There are always exceptions, however. For some species only very young, pliable material will form roots. If in doubt as to the proper ripeness of the wood, take cuttings immediately after the shrub has bloomed and several times thereafter at two-week intervals. This is practical, of course, only if the plant is easily accessible. Avoid collecting stems that either have extremely weak growth or excessively vigorous growth. They may fail to root or may produce frail plants.

Summer cuttings of softwood or half-ripened wood wilt quickly, so gather together all the materials you need before you start. Collect cuttings in a damp plastic bag, preferably in early morning when the stems are full of water and before the leaves become wilted in the hot sun. Immediately insert them in the propagating bed. If necessary, you can keep cuttings in a cool place for a few hours and they will stay fresh.

Because root-producing chemicals are stored in the tip of the bud and travel quickly to the cut end, it is important to trim shoots to size as they are collected. The length of a stem cutting varies with the type of plant material, but as a general rule the length should not exceed four inches. Use a sharp knife to cut the shoot at a slight angle just below a *leaf node* (the point where the leaf joins the stem).

Remove leaves and thorns from the part of the cutting that will come in contact with the soil. Also remove spent flowers and flower buds, which drain energy needed for root formation. To encourage more rapid root growth, you can wound the stem at the base by using a sharp razor blade to remove a one-half- to one-inch-long strip of the outer layer of wood. This step is not necessary if the stem is very small or fragile.

On shrubs that develop many short, side branchlets from a main stem, pull each shoot down and off the main stem, leaving a "heel" of old wood at the base of the cutting. These are called *heel cuttings*. Trim the excess wood at the heel and wound the stem in the same manner as on a stem cutting.

A standard-sized (fourteen by sixteen by four inches) wooden flat that is used by nurseries will hold many cuttings. You can substitute shallow, wooden fruit boxes, which can be obtained from the grocery store, or you can go to a lumber yard and buy one-quarter-inch thick fir lumber that can be cut to size and nailed together. It is important to allow for drainage by leaving one-eighth-inch wide spaces between the boards on the bottom of the box or by drilling small holes in the wood. If you are preparing only a few cuttings, use a clay pot or a one-pound coffee can.

Fill the flat or pot with the rooting medium. The preferred medium is one part peat and three parts coarse sand, well mixed. Perlite or vermiculite are good substitutes for peat. All of these materials retain the moisture the cuttings need yet allow air to penetrate to the stem ends that will sprout roots. Soak the flat thoroughly with water, let it drain,

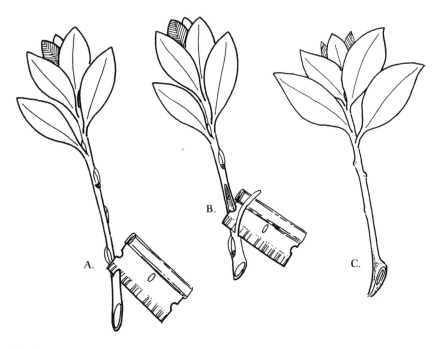

Cuttings.
    A. Stem cutting. The length of a stem cutting should not exceed four inches; it should be cut at a slight angle just below a leaf node.
    B. Wounding the stem. Remove a thin, one-half- to one-inch long strip of the outer layer of wood.
    C. Heel cutting. Pull a side shoot from the main stem of a plant, leaving a heel of old wood at the base of the cutting.

then tamp the soil with a brick or small block of wood to firm it and remove air pockets. The flat is now ready to receive the cuttings.

Dip the cut end of the stem into a mixture of *root-inducing hormone*, which speeds up rooting activity, and *fungicide*, which protects the cuttings from fungal diseases. The hormone and fungicide are available in both solution and powder forms and can be purchased at garden centers.

Use a nail or small wood round to make a hole in the soil. Insert the cutting about two inches in the soil and space the cuttings in rows one to two inches apart. If the leaves are very large, you may cut off half the leaf in order to keep the cutting from losing too much moisture through the large leaf area. Leaves that have a tendency to droop can be bundled and held upright with a rubber band to keep them from touching the soil or shading the other cuttings. Gently firm the soil around each cutting. After you place the last cutting, moisten the leaves and settle the soil with a fine spray of water. Label each species of plant material with a plastic label, using a waterproof felt pen so that the identification remains legible in outdoor weather conditions.

The best way to maintain an even humidity around the cuttings is to enclose the container in a tent of clear plastic. A half-hoop of wire at each end of the flat will hold the plastic a few inches above the tops of the cuttings and allow air circulation. Secure the plastic firmly around the edge of the flat with cord and fold the loose ends of the plastic underneath the flat.

Store the cuttings in a warm, light, sheltered place that is out of direct sunlight. Check the flat every few days to be certain it contains an even moisture, and keep it clean by picking out any fallen, decaying leaves.

The time it takes for cuttings to root varies considerably. Some species root within three or four weeks while others may require a much longer period, even as long as a year. For reasons unknown, a few will disappoint you and will not take root at all.

An alternative to leaving the cuttings at the mercy of nature's temperature changes is to give the cutting flat bottom heat. One method is to use a *propagating mat*, which plugs into a standard electrical outlet and is regulated by a thermostat control. The mat can be placed on the ground, on cement outdoors, or on a cement floor indoors. The advantage of using a propagating mat is that, inside the covered flat, the temperature and humidity remain constant, which causes quicker rooting and a better percentage of rooting success. If you need large quantities of plants in your landscape plan, the propagating mat will pay

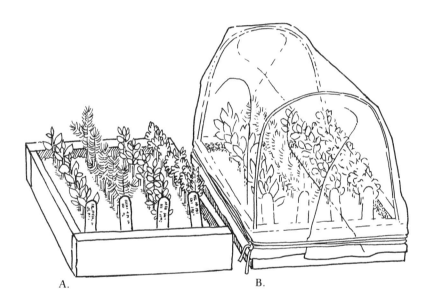

Cutting flat.
  A. Insert cuttings two inches deep in the soil and space the cuttings in rows one to two inches apart.
  B. Maintain humidity around the cuttings by enclosing the flat in a tent of clear plastic.

for itself many times over by hastening the rooting time for cuttings, probably by as much as half the time that is necessary under natural conditions. It is safe, convenient, and inexpensive to use and will hold many flats of cuttings or seeds because the flats may be stacked three or four deep. Be sure, however, that they are offset in order to allow air circulation. Temperatures between sixty and seventy degrees Fahrenheit are recommended for bottom heat for cuttings and seeds. Propagating mats are available from garden centers or nursery supply companies.

Potting

As soon as the cuttings form several robust roots, remove them from the flat and place them in individual pots so they will receive the nutrients necessary for top growth. A good general potting medium is one part peat, one part sand, and two parts rich garden soil mixed together thoroughly. If you do not have these ingredients readily accessible, you may find it more convenient to use the packaged potting soil available at garden centers.

Use three- or four-inch-diameter clay or plastic pots that have drainage holes in the bottom. If the pots have been used previously, scrub them in soapy water, then rinse and drain them. Remember that soil does not dry out so quickly in plastic pots as it does in clay containers.

Place soil in the bottom half of a pot and firm the soil with your hand or with a wooden block. Use a table fork to lift the rooted cutting carefully from the flat and transfer it to the pot. Dribble soil around the roots and tamp gently, being careful not to damage the tender roots; leave an inch of space from the soil level to the top of the pot to allow for adding water. As each rooted cutting is potted, set each pot in a pan of water until the soil is thoroughly moistened.

Cold Frame

Once the cuttings are potted, place them in a shaded cold frame and keep them there until the following spring or fall, or until they have developed a sturdy root system. Keeping the newly potted plants watered is important. If you allow the fragile roots to become dry and withered, they will be unable to transport water and nutrients to the rest of the plant and the plant will die.

If your locality is subject to frost or deep freezing, protect the young plants by sinking the pots completely in sand, soil, or bark mulch and keep the cold frame covered with burlap or plastic. In regions where winters are severe, you can put the cold frame against the house where it will receive some warmth from the house.

If you do not already have a cold frame, you can quite easily build a

New roots are fragile. Use a table fork to lift the cutting and transfer it to a pot.

wooden frame that will last for many years. (Brick or concrete can be used instead, but are more expensive.) In most regions, scrap fir lumber is readily available and can be used to construct the sides and cover of the frame. It needs no bottom as the frame rests on the soil. You can make the frame as small or as large as needed to hold the plants. I prefer a size that is thirty inches by seven feet, and two feet high at the back and eighteen inches high at the front. Drill a few small holes in each side to allow air circulation through the structure when the cover is closed. If the frame is a very small size, you can place a sheet of clear plastic over the top and fasten it to the sides with cord or thumbtacks. If the frame is larger, it is more convenient to use a slatted cover that is hinged at one end. During summer, the slatted cover furnishes shade for the plants. When winter arrives, a clear-plastic sheet or burlap can be placed over the slatted cover to protect the plants from the cold.

Moving the Plant to the Garden

Some species of plants grow rapidly and are ready to be planted in their permanent location after a year. The width and depth of the hole you dig depends on the size of the plant. Figure the amount of space to be filled by the roots, then add at least eight inches all around the plant and about twelve inches below the roots. To allow good drainage, put a one- or two-inch layer of sand and coarse gravel at the bottom of the hole and then add garden soil mix.

Set the shrub in the hole atop a mixture of two parts garden soil and one part peat so that the shrub's soil line is about one inch below the surface of the ground. If the plant is heavily rooted, carefully spread the roots so they reach out toward the sides of the hole. Fill the hole three-fourths full with garden soil mix and tamp the soil down with your hands. Fill the remaining space with water. When the water has drained away, again fill the hole completely with soil and water. A two- or three-inch dike of soil mounded around the hole will hold the water so it soaks in around the plant rather than running off. During the first year or two when it is becoming established, the plant will need plenty of moisture to encourage healthy, vigorous root growth, but it must have good drainage in order to avoid root rot. During the hot summer season, it may be necessary to water the plant daily.

A light mulch of sawdust, ground bark, or gravel retains soil moisture and will protect the tender roots from winter frosts. Another precaution is to place a screen or several rocks around the small plant to keep it from being trampled. Once the wild shrub has established a sturdy root system and healthy top growth, it will require little attention.

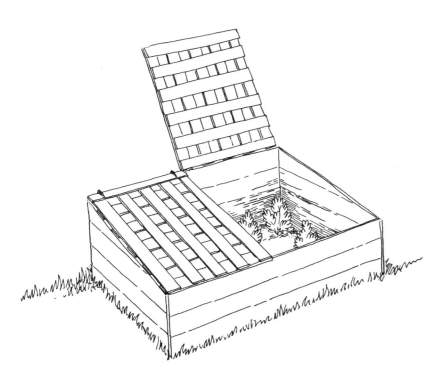

One style of cold frame has a slatted cover, hinged at one side, that provides shade and protection for young plants.

Fertilizer

If you plant a shrub properly, it will need no additional fertilizer. However, if it does not seem to be growing well a few months after it has been planted, scatter a small amount of fertilizer on the surface beneath the plant and water it in. The fertilizer you should use depends on the requirements of the shrub. You can give plants that need an acid soil a standard compound that is labeled "rhododendron-azalea-camellia fertilizer." This is a fast-acting chemical that acidifies the soil as it feeds. For plants that prefer a nonacid soil, a good fast-acting fertilizer is one that is labeled "5-10-5," which has relative proportions of nitrogen, phosphorus, and potassium. You apply both the acid and nonacid compounds in early spring. Using fast-acting fertilizers in late summer may stimulate growth that can be damaged by cold fall weather. You can apply slow-acting organic fertilizers, such as bone meal or cottonseed meal, in late fall or early spring. *Be sparing, however, in using fertilizer on wild shrubs.* Overfeeding can burn the roots of small plants and weaken or kill them, and may cause abnormal, leggy growth in older plants.

Seed Propagation

Under conditions in the wild, most shrubs are dependent on seeds for their reproduction. When seeds ripen and fall to the ground, they may be covered by leaves, scattered by the wind, floated down streams and left in muddy banks, buried by animals, or carried many miles by birds. Although nature is extravagant with seeds, only a small percentage land in places that are favorable to germination. Much can be learned by observing the conditions under which seeds do germinate and grow in the wild.

Propagating wild shrubs from seeds is not just a simple matter of scattering them over the ground. Some seeds are slow to germinate and once sprouted, are slow to mature. Certain seeds require special handling to ensure satisfactory germination. This may involve removing their pulpy covering, storing them at low temperatures to bring about changes that are essential to germination, or cracking or filing the heavy protective shells to allow moisture to penetrate to the seeds' embryos. It is also in nature's design that plants raised from seeds may differ from the parent plant because new genetic traits are introduced during the process of pollination by insects.

Regardless of a few difficulties that may be encountered, seed propagation is another good method of bringing wild shrubs into your garden. Pick the seed pods in the fall after they have turned brown but before they have split open to discharge seeds. Put the pods of different

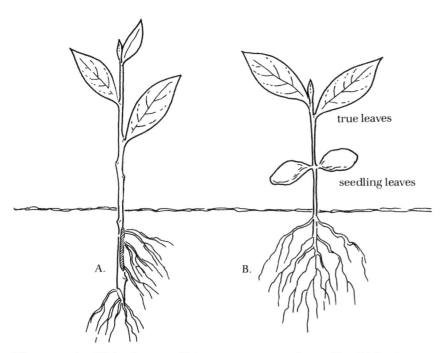

When a cutting (A) develops a sufficient root system and a seedling (B) develops its true leaves, the young plants must be transplanted to richer soil so the roots and leaves can obtain the nutrients necessary for growth.

species in separate envelopes, mark each envelope with the name of its plant, and store them in a cool, dry place until you are ready to plant the seeds. Seeds from wild shrubs are best planted outdoors in late fall or winter. They will germinate in the early spring when the moisture and temperature are right to trigger action in the embryo.

In an outdoor planting, prepare a small plot of good soil in an area that is protected from frost and wind. Plant the seeds a few inches apart and cover them with a thin layer of soil or fine sand, just deep enough to keep them moist. If they are covered with too much soil, the food stored in the seed will be exhausted before the growing stem reaches the surface. You can more easily handle tiny, dustlike seeds by sowing them in flats or small pots. Once the seeds are sown, it is essential to keep the medium moist because seeds in the germination stage are tender and quickly die if they dry out. To water them, sprinkle a very fine mist on the soil or set the pots or flats in a shallow pan of water and remove them when moisture appears on the surface. After the seeds are sown, treat the surface of the seed bed with a fungicide to prevent a fungus-caused rot called *damping off*. Place a netting or wire screen a few inches above the seed bed to keep squirrels, birds, and domestic animals from damaging the plot. This also keeps leaves and other coarse debris from smothering the seed bed.

When the sprouted seedlings have developed their *true leaves*, which come after the initial pair of seedling leaves, transplant them into pots and set them in a shaded cold frame until they are large enough to plant in the garden. Give the seedlings the same care as that recommended for rooted cuttings.

Ground Layering

In ground layering, the plant to be propagated should have flexible branches that can be brought down to the ground and held there until sufficient roots are formed on the layers to permit them to be cut from the parent plant. At the point of contact between the branch and the soil, dig a broad trench about six inches deep. Bend the stem to touch the ground about a foot from the tip. Use a sharp knife to cut a small slit at the bend and keep the slit open by inserting a matchstick or similar-sized stick. Dust the cut with root-inducing hormone powder. Hold the cut portion in the trench and cover it with three or four inches of soil that consists of equal parts of coarse sand and damp peat. A rock placed over the layer keeps the branch in place and helps conserve moisture in the soil.

Ground layering is a convenient method of increasing plants by rooting branches while they are still attached to the parent plant.

A year later the layer should have a good root system. Cut it from the parent stem and transplant it to its permanent place in the garden. Because of the rooting time involved, this kind of propagation is practical only if the shrub is easily accessible to you.

Suckers, Stolons, and Runners

Some shrubs put a "best foot forward" to increase their species. From the main plant, they send out stems or roots that creep beneath or above the ground's surface in an ever widening circle from the parent shrub. A new plant eventually sprouts.

A *sucker* is a shoot that starts below the ground from the root or an underground stem. Examples of plants that bear these specialized shoots are salal (*Gaultheria shallon*) and the Oregon grapes (*Berberis aquifolium* and *B. nervosa*).

A shoot that starts above the surface of the ground and then bends over so that it comes in contact with the soil and forms roots is called a *stolon* or *runner*. Red osier dogwood (*Cornus stolonifera*) forms dense thickets by this means, as does the miniature, trailing raspberry (*Rubus pedatus*). These shoots provide an easy means of propagating the plants. Cut the sucker or stolon that runs between plants, dig up the rooted shoots in late fall or early spring, and transplant them to your garden in the same way you transplant rooted cuttings.

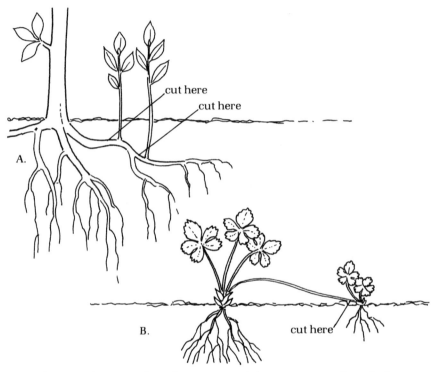

Transplant a sucker (A) and a stolon or runner (B) to permanent places in the garden by cutting them from their main stems.

Plant Names and Identification

Plant Names

Potentilla fruticosa is known by several common English names: shrubby cinquefoil, yellow rose, and rock rose. In the western United States, *Amelanchier alnifolia* is referred to as serviceberry, while in the eastern states it is called shadbush because it blooms at the time the shad fish begin to ascend the tidal rivers. Sticky laurel, mountain balm, cinnamon bush, tobacco bush, and greasewood are common names of *Ceanothus velutinus*. To add to the confusion, a common name is often applied to two or more different plants. Greasewood is another name for a desert shrub called *Sarcobatus vermiculatus*, which is unrelated to *Ceanothus velutinus*.

Very few of the common English names designate the same plant throughout the world. Some originated as an old folk-name, a chance designation, translation of a Latin botanical name, or names coined by people who feel that botanical names are too technical. Most of these English names are misleading or erroneous and only add more confusion when you attempt to identify a specific plant that grows in many localities.

The need for an organized system to identify plants was recognized by the Swedish botanist Carolus Linnaeus. His book *Species Plantarum* (published in 1753) was the starting point for a system of priority that divides all plants into classes, orders, families, genera, and species based on sexuality in flowering plants. Since the mid-eighteenth century, botanists have continued to develop this system of arrangement and correlate the natural relationships among plants.

As the number of plants known to man increased, botanists gradually adopted an international standard of naming plants and plant groups. This work is accomplished at a meeting known as the International Congress, which is held every four years. The rules and regulations adopted and published by this Congress are known as the *International Code of Botanical Nomenclature*. All plants, worldwide, are classified and given their scientific names in accordance with this code.

The scientific name of any plant is in two parts—the name of the genus and the species name. These designations are Latin names or are names taken from some other language and latinized.

The generic name may describe a prominent characteristic in the included species, the original name of the plant, or a name in honor of a person. It is a singular noun and is always written with a capital initial letter. *Pachistima*, the generic name of *Pachistima myrsinites* (mountain box), is derived from the Greek words *pachys*, meaning "thick," and *stigma*, which refers to the part of the flower that receives the pollen grains. Thus, the genus name describes the thick stigma that is a prominent characteristic of the plant.

The specific name may refer to the locality where the species was first discovered, describe the plant, portray its habitat, or honor a person. It is written with the initial letter in the lower case. The botanical name *Corylus cornuta* (hazelnut) is derived from the Latin *korys*, meaning "helmet," and *cornuta*, meaning "horned." Both the genus and the species names describe the distinctive shape of the hard-shelled calyx that encloses the seeds of this plant.

Where subdivisions in species need to be shown, several designations are used in their descending order of magnitude: subspecies, variety, and form. Form is usually associated with minor differences caused by environment. Subspecies and varieties are based on differences that are caused by heredity, environment, geology, and other factors. An example of variation is in black elderberry—*Sambucus racemosa* variety (or "var.") *melanocarpa*—which differs from the red elderberry—*Sambucus racemosa* variety *arborescens*—by producing black berries and by exhibiting growing habit differences, which are caused by its limited geographical location.

Related genera are further grouped into a family. Only rarely is there a single genus in a family. The family name, except for a few that antedate the standardized system, is a plural adjective formed by adding "aceae" to the stem of a legitimate generic name. For example, "Ericaceae" is from *Erica*, "Rosaceae" from *Rosa*. This designation was originally defined by Carolus Linnaeus.

A botanical name is exact. It applies to only one kind of plant and that same plant is known by its two-part name (or *binomial*) around the

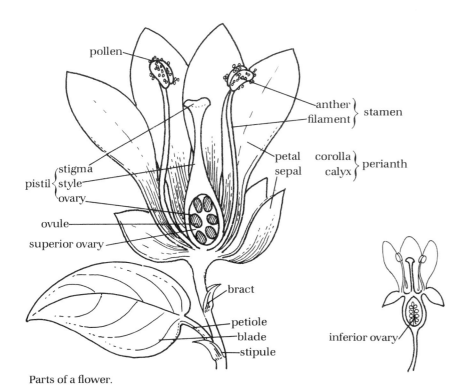

Parts of a flower.

world. For that reason, this book always includes the Latin name for each plant mentioned. However, to make it easier for those who are not acquainted with these botanical names, a common English name is also used. In addition, this book uses the *Englerian sequence*, which classifies plants in families on the basis of origin and relationship. For convenience of reference, the genera within each family and the species within each genera are in alphabetical order.

Written after the scientific name of the plant is the name of the person, or occasionally two or more persons, who originally published an account of the plant and described and named it. The author's name may be written out completely, but more often it is indicated by a standardized abbreviation (see "Authors' Names Used in Botanical Designations"). *Garrya elliptica*, for example, was first named and described by the botanist David Douglas and is written as *Garrya elliptica* Dougl.

Whenever some change in nomenclature is made, the name of the original author is placed in parentheses and is followed by the name of the person making the change. *Cassiope mertensiana* (Bong.) D. Don was first designated and published under the name *Andromeda mertensiana* by Heinrich Bongard and later reclassified to the genus *Cassiope* by David Don.

Plant Identification

Stem forms, leaf structures, and flower parts are the characteristics by which flowering plants are most readily distinguished, and in the science of botany there is a technical terminology that describes the various features.

Stems may be quite diverse in size and texture and may differ in the direction in which they grow. Sometimes they are modified for special functions. Stolons, for instance, trail above the ground, take root at the leaf nodes, and produce new plants. All other features of a plant originate on the stem from buds that develop into leaves, branches, and new stem growth.

A leaf may consist of three main parts: the *blade* or enlarged portion, the *petiole* or leaf stalk, and the *stipules*, which are a pair of appendages at the base of the petiole. A single blade is called a *simple leaf*; but if a leaf has more than one blade, it is a *compound leaf* and the blades are called *leaflets*. The leaflets, in turn, are described by other names depending on their shape and arrangement. Another feature that is important to observe is the *margin*, or edge of the leaf blade. Variance in the margins of leaves on different plants is described in terms such as *wavy, toothed*, *lobed, serrate,* or other expressions that relate to its character. Other distinguishing characteristics are the veins of a leaf and the texture of the leaf surface.

An *inflorescence* is the arrangement of flowers on a plant. This may be a simple arrangement of a single blossom or it may be a complex structure that includes several dozen flowers. An arrangement of numerous flowers may take the form of a *panicle, raceme, spike, corymb, head, umbel,* or *catkin.*

Features of an individual flower include the placement, size, and color of its various parts: *sepals, petals, stamens,* and *pistils.* There is a great variety in forms of flowers, but the following description of a typical flower will provide some understanding of the separate features and the botanical terms used to describe those features. At the base of a typical flower is a green cup that is split into five segments. The structure as a whole is the *calyx* and each segment is a *sepal.* Above or within the calyx is the *corolla* or colored portion of the flower. It is split into five *lobes* and each lobe is called a *petal.*

Within the corolla there are five slender stalks, each topped with a head that is covered with powdery masses. These are the *stamens* or male reproductive organs. The stalks are called *filaments* and the heads are *anthers*, which carry the pollen. In the center of the flower, there is a flask-shaped structure called the *pistil*, which is the female reproductive organ. The bulbous base of the pistil is the *ovary,* which contains the *ovules*; after fertilization, they become the *seeds.* The stalk of the pistil is the *style* and the expanded tip is the *stigma.*

The language of plants is not so awesome as it may at first appear. Many of the words are already a part of the average gardener's vocabulary. Studying the glossary and diagrams of plant features for a few hours will familiarize you with the botanical terms and enable you more easily to identify a wild shrub in the field.

Forty Wild Shrubs

In the following pages, you will find detailed information about forty of the Northwest's most easily grown, flowering, wild shrubs. The botanical information is presented in the form in which botanists use it, but can easily be understood by laymen. In addition, general information, landscaping ideas, name originations, and growing tips provide you with all the essentials for bringing these shrubs into your garden scheme.

Myrica californica Cham.   **Myricaceae**
Wax myrtle   **Sweet Gale Family**

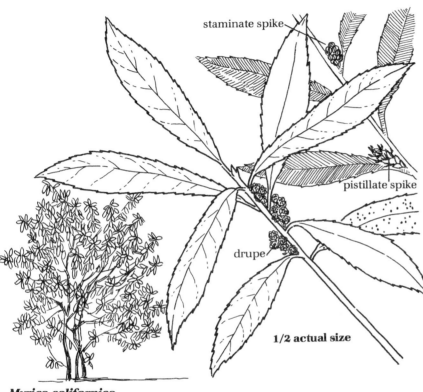

Myrica californica

Propagation: Cuttings from May to August, or seeds.
Height: 2 to 6 m; occasionally to 10 m.
Leaves: Alternate, simple, evergreen. Blades elliptic or elliptic-oblanceolate, 5 to 15 cm long, mostly toothed above the middle, leathery, finely black-dotted.
Flowers: Monoecious. Brown, staminate spikes about 5 mm long, pistillate spikes 1 to 2 cm long. The pistillate catkins are above the staminate catkins. Some catkins contain both staminate and pistillate parts. Stamens 3 to 12. Ovary, 1-celled.
Bloom: April to May.
Fruit: Drupe, purplish, 4 to 8 mm long, wax-coated.
Range: Vancouver Island to California.

Wax myrtle is a close-branched, evergreen shrub that sometimes grows in the form of a small tree up to thirty feet tall. Young twigs are hairy and finely covered with wax lenticels, but become smooth with age; the leaves, too, are resinous, or waxy, and have black-dotted glands. Its spring-blooming flowers are inconspicuous, as are its small, brown catkins. Staminate and pistillate catkins are on the same plant.

Wax myrtle's sweet, spicy scent is described by its genus name, which comes from the Greek word *myrike*, meaning "to perfume." The plant is of value as an ornamental because of this spicy aroma, its neat year-round appearance, and glossy, dark green leaves. Deer browse the twigs and foliage, and birds and small mammals eat the wax-coated fruit.

Like sweet gale (*Myrica gale*), wax myrtle inhabits lake shores, stream banks, and bogs; in cultivation, it requires acid, moist (but well-drained) soil, and either full sun or shade. The plant grows easily and needs little pruning if it is given enough space to grow to its maximum size, and thus is useful as an informal or clipped hedge, or as a screen. The best method of propagation is to plant seeds. Remove all the wax from the fruits but do not allow them to dry. Seeds will germinate if they are planted outdoors in early fall.

Myrica gale L.
Sweet gale

Myricaceae
Sweet Gale Family

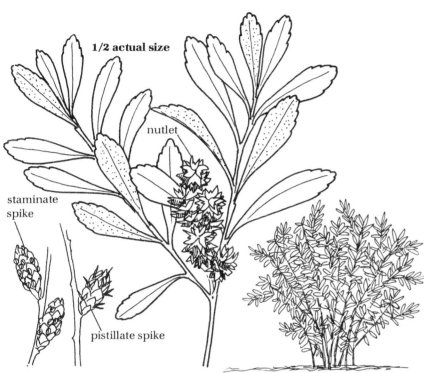

Myrica gale
Propagation: Cuttings from May to August, seeds, or layering.
Height: 0.5 to 2 m.
Leaves: Alternate, simple, deciduous. Blades oblanceolate, 3 to 6 cm long, coarse teeth near tip, hairy, and dotted with bright yellow wax glands on both surfaces.
Flowers: Dioecious. Brown, flowers are small, without sepals or petals, unisexual in short scaly spikes. Staminate spikes 1 to 2 cm long. Pistillate spikes about half as long as the staminate. Stamens 3 to 5, enclosed in stacked scales. Bractlets exceed the pistil and are fused with it at the base. Ovary, 1-celled.
Bloom: April to June.
Fruit: Nutlet, green, 2-winged, 3 mm long, wax-coated.
Range: Alaska to Newfoundland, south to British Columbia, northwest Oregon, Michigan, Wisconsin, Virginia; and in Appalachian Mountains to Tennessee and North Carolina.

Sweet gale is one of the earliest-blooming plants at the edge of tidal flats, in coastal swamps, and in bogs from the lowlands to high elevations. By means of suckering roots, this loosely branched shrub forms large thickets about four feet tall. When young, its slender twigs are finely hairy, then turn dark brown to gray and, when mature, become covered with yellow resin dots and white dots (lenticels). Before leaves are evident, staminate and pistillate catkins develop on different plants. When the catkins ripen, air movement or the touch of insects releases clouds of yellow pollen. It is a deciduous plant, erect and stiff in form, with alternate leaves that have a spicy odor.

The sweet gale of the Northwest is a fragrant shrub that is similar to the eastern species of bayberry (*M. carolinensis*), a source of wax used in scented candles since colonial times. Its name is derived from the Greek word *myrike*, which refers to the aroma of the leaves.

Sweet gale grows well in cultivation if it has wet, peaty soil and sun. Because the flowers are dioecious, fruiting plants require a male plant in their midst. As a landscape shrub, it is not so valuable as the evergreen wax myrtle (*M. californica*), but the spicy perfume from its leaves is a pleasing addition to other garden fragrances.

***Corylus cornuta* Marsh.**
Hazelnut, filbert

Betulaceae
Birch Family

No woodland garden should be without at least one hazelnut, a shrub that is so common (its several varieties grow throughout North America) that its beauty is not fully appreciated. It is most visible in late winter when, long before leaves appear, alderlike catkins hang like slender icicles from the graceful, arching branches. These light brown catkins are the staminate flowers; a close look at the branch reveals the dark red pistillate flower. Later in the year, a pair of bractlets surrounds the maturing ovary and forms a hairy involucre around the nut. The nuts often grow base to base in pairs, as in the winged fruit (samara) of the western maple tree.

Indians and pioneers ground hazelnuts into flour. Nowadays, hybridized species are commercially cultivated under the name "filbert" (a common name for the European species), and are high in calories, fats, and proteins. The fertile valleys in northwestern Oregon sustain many acres of commercially grown filberts.

The botanical name describes the shape of the calyx that encloses the nut. *Corylus* is from the Latin *korys* ("helmet") and *cornuta* ("horned").

Squirrels and jays harvest the brown nuts even before they are ripe. Steller's jays have a special fondness for the meaty kernel inside each nut; when a shell is too hard for a jay to crack, he tucks the nut under soil in a rockery, planter box, cutting flat, or any similar hiding place. In late winter, a pounding on the rooftop at daybreak is a signal that the jay is breaking his softened hazelnut. Because jays do not remember all the hiding places, two-leaved sprouts begin popping out of the ground by

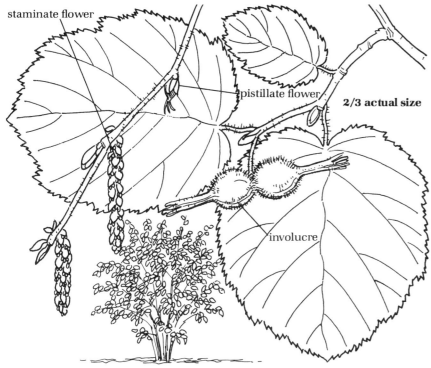

June in various corners of the garden. Perhaps jays do not forget the nuts but plant a few to ensure a supply of hazelnuts for their future generations. If Steller's jays visit your garden, watch for their sprouted nuts and move the seedlings to protected locations.

Propagate hazelnuts by planting mature nuts outside where the soil is moist. Transplant the sprouted nuts the following summer. The shrub finds almost any location suitable—it is not particular about soil and thrives in either sun or shade. Hazelnut is effective in the landscape when planted near a fence where it forms a background for smaller shrubs, or as a grouping on a steep bank.

Corylus cornuta
Propagation: Seeds.
Height: 1 to 5 m.
Leaves: Alternate, simple, deciduous. Blades oval-oblong, 4 to 10 cm long, finely toothed, hairy.
Flowers: Staminate flowers in slender, brown catkins, 4 to 7 cm long. Pistillate flowers with dark red stigmas clustered in a scaly bud. Flowers appear before leaves. Stamens 8. Ovary inferior, 1-celled.
Bloom: January to March.
Fruit: Hard-shelled nut, 1.5 cm long, enclosed in an involucre.
Range: Widespread in the Northwest; variations of the species grow throughout North America.

***Berberis aquifolium* Pursh**
Tall Oregon grape, mahonia

Berberidaceae
Barberry Family

Tall Oregon grape is common in woods and sagebrush slopes of its range, but this does not lessen its considerable merit as a garden specimen. Its beauty, hardiness, and popularity were recognized when it was chosen to be Oregon's state flower. In early spring, the pinkish bronze new growth of terminal leaves blends with older, dark green, glossy foliage to form a varicolored background for splendid, bright yellow flowers. The shrub produces another spectacle in midsummer when its grapelike clusters of berries turn dark blue. These berries make a tasty jelly and a dark red, rich, fruity wine.

A broken stem reveals a feature that is unique to the Oregon grape species: bright yellow inner bark. Some Indian tribes boiled the roots and bark to obtain yellow dye for basketry materials.

The genus comes from the Arabic name *berberys*, meaning "plant." *Aquifolium* is descriptive of wet or shining leaves. In the Northwest, Oregon grape is better known by horticulturalists and nurserymen as the genus *Mahonia*. Tall Oregon grape, because of its thornless stems and evergreen, pinnate leaves, has been placed in the separate genus *Mahonia* by some botanists. However, there are no constant genetic differences, so taxonomically Oregon grape is considered as a section of the genus *Berberis*.

Tall Oregon grape is a versatile evergreen ornamental, usually of erect, bushy habit. In a mass planting, it can hide an unattractive fence or concrete wall, or you can prune and train it in order to make a thick hedge that delineates property lines, separates driveways, or serves as a

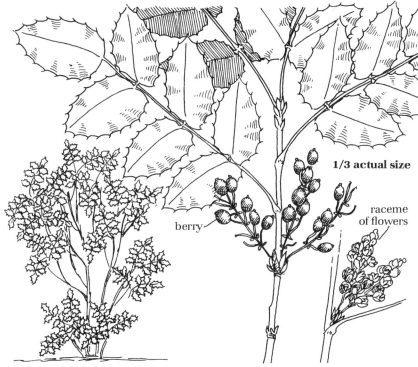

Berberis aquifolium

Propagation: Cuttings from May to August, seeds, layering, or suckers.
Height: 2 to 45 dm.
Leaves: Alternate, pinnate, leaflets 5 to 9, evergreen. Blades oblong to ovate, 3 to 8 cm long, coarsely toothed with spines, veined, glossy green above, paler beneath.
Flowers: Bright yellow, in racemes 3 to 8 cm long, clustered in leaf axils and on end of stem. Ovary superior, 1-celled.
Bloom: March to May.
Fruit: Berry, dark blue, 7 to 14 mm long.
Range: British Columbia to northern California, from coast to Idaho.

barrier between street and garden. This fine shrub grows abundantly in Oregon where park administrators wisely leave it and other native trees and shrubs to form natural, effective, attractive screens among the campsites.

Prune Oregon grape lightly in winter to keep it tidy and healthy and to encourage new growth. About every other year, severely cut back old woody stems that extend high above the foliage. Fresh growth starts from the base and rapidly fills any open spaces. Because Oregon grape spreads freely by suckers, take the precaution of planting the shrub where its invasive suckers do not grow over less aggressive shrubs.

A prostrate species of Oregon grape, *Berberis repens*, grows east of the Cascade Mountains. It is similar to *B. aquifolium* and has leaflets (usually five to seven) and leaf edges that are less prominently spiny toothed. New plants start where the trailing stems touch the ground and form roots.

***Berberis nervosa* Pursh**
**Low Oregon grape,
low mahonia**

**Berberidaceae
Barberry Family**

A long, erect stem that bears hollylike leaves immediately identifies low Oregon grape—there is little chance to confuse it with any other native shrub. West of the Cascades, it is a common ground cover that displays little variation in shape and thrives in filtered shade under taller shrubs and trees. Surprisingly, deer and rabbits browse the prickly foliage.

New leaves are a delicate bronze color until they mature and turn dark green and develop a leathery texture. Often, the older leaves are edged with maroon, and sometimes a leaf will turn brilliant red. Blue berries that ripen in late summer are similar in size and color to those of salal (*Gaultheria shallon*), but they are slightly more tart and make excellent jelly and wine.

The species name, *nervosa*, means "veined." The generic name is from the Arabic word *berberys*, which means "plant." Because Oregon grape has evergreen, pinnate leaves and thornless stems, some botanists have placed it in the separate genus *Mahonia*, and many northwest horticulturalists and botanists know the plant by this genus. However, there are no constant genetic differences, so taxonomically Oregon grape is considered as a section of the genus *Berberis*.

Clusters of blue fruit; attractive leaves; and bright yellow, early blooming, long lasting flowers make low Oregon grape one of the best native shrubs for year-round beauty in the garden. It is unexcelled as a low-maintenance ground cover because it suffocates weeds and requires

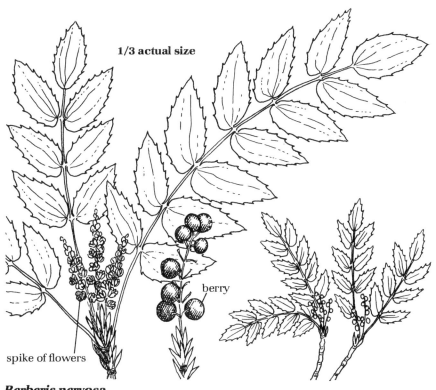

no pruning or special care. It is most desirable when planted in masses and allowed to spread by its natural method of suckers. Combine it with conifers and tall, broad-leaved, evergreen shrubs where it will receive filtered light and protection from wind.

Berberis nervosa

Propagation: Cuttings from June to August, seeds, or suckers.
Height: 1 to 6 dm.
Leaves: Alternate, pinnate, leaflets 7 to 21, evergreen. Blades ovate-lanceolate, 3 to 6 cm long, coarsely toothed with slender spines, stiff, veined.
Flowers: Yellow, in spikes 7 to 18 cm long, several arising from 1 bud. Ovary superior, 1-celled.
Bloom: March to June.
Fruit: Berry, deep blue with whitish bloom, 8 to 11 mm long.
Range: British Columbia to central California, west of Cascade Mountains.

***Ribes sanguineum* Pursh** **Grossulariaceae**
Red currant, red flowering **Gooseberry and**
currant, blood currant **Currant Family**

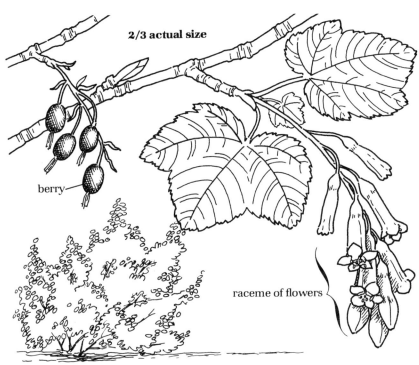

Ribes sanguineum
Propagation: Cuttings from June to August, seeds, or layering.
Height: 1 to 3 m.
Leaves: Alternate, simple, deciduous. Blades reniform or cordate-orbicular, 2.5 to 6 cm broad, 3- to 5-lobed, irregularly toothed, deeply veined, dark green above, paler and hairy beneath.
Flowers: Pink to deep red, 3 to 4 mm long, 10 to 20 flowers in a raceme. Corolla 5 petals. Stamens 5. Ovary inferior, 1-celled.
Bloom: March to June.
Fruit: Berry, black, covered with whitish bloom, 7 to 9 mm long, many-seeded.
Range: British Columbia to middle coast ranges of California, from coast to east slopes of Cascade Mountains.

Among the many species of currants that grow in the wild, the red currant is the most attractive when in flower. In early spring, the long, arching branches—weighted with clusters of bright, rosy pink blossoms—bend toward the ground. Its species name means "blood-red," which refers to the color of the flowers. The genus name is from the Arabic word *ribas*, meaning "the plant." Its reddish brown bark, lack of thorns, and five-lobed, veined leaves distinguish red currant from other species of *Ribes*.

Red currant is not only one of the most beautiful native shrubs to use for ornamental purposes, but it also thrives in cultivation. It is not selective in habitat and grows as readily in dry, rocky, exposed situations as it does in moist, open woods. Full exposure to sunlight encourages it, in the spring, to produce a heavy cascade of bloom that lasts for nearly a month. After blooming, red currant requires only a light pruning to maintain its neat habit. Its shapeliness and colorful bloom make it desirable in a background planting (perhaps against a cedar fence) or as a specimen in a rockery.

Although it is free of insect pests, red currant has one undesirable quality: the genus harbors white pine blister rust and this lovely shrub may become a villain if white pines are growing in the immediate neighborhood.

***Philadelphus lewisii* Pursh**
Mock orange

Hydrangeaceae
Hydrangea Family

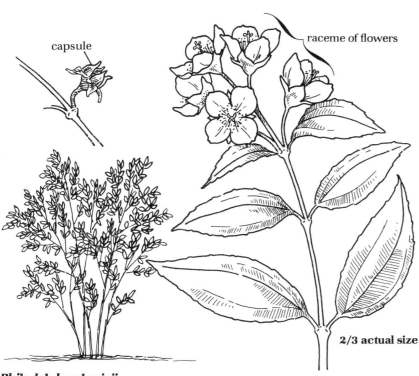

Philadelphus lewisii
- **Propagation:** Cuttings from August to September, or suckers from old plants.
- **Height:** 1.5 to 3 m.
- **Leaves:** Opposite, simple, deciduous. Blades ovate to ovate-lanceolate, 2.5 to 7 cm long, entire to slightly toothed, 3 to 5 conspicuous veins from near the base.
- **Flowers:** White, 10 to 20 mm long, 3 to 11 in terminal racemes on lateral branches, also axillary. Corolla 4 or 5 petals. Stamens 25 to 40. Ovary inferior, 4-celled.
- **Bloom:** May to July.
- **Fruit:** Capsule, 6 to 10 mm long, splits into 4 valves.
- **Range:** British Columbia to northern California, from coast to Rocky Mountains.

Mock orange bears a profusion of white blossoms that often exude a slightly orangelike fragrance. This erect shrub is distinguished from similar-sized, white-flowering shrubs by its pairs of opposite branchlets and thin, scaling bark. The showy flowers are succeeded by seed capsules that persist in winter.

Environment is of little concern to mock orange. It grows equally well in river valleys or on dry, rocky cliffs, and associates with such durable members of the plant kingdom as sagebrush, pine, fir, and redwood.

The generic name commemorates the Pharaoh Ptolemy II Philadelphus (308-246 B.C.), king of Egypt. The species, *lewisii*, refers to the famous northwest explorer Captain Meriwether Lewis.

Mock orange has a stiff, unshapely form and leaves that cling late and finally fall with little change of color. But its spectacular white bloom more than qualifies it for a place in the woodland garden. Mock orange's white beauty is most effective when the plant is combined with other shrubs to form a background for a mass of multicolored roses or other large-flowered plants that bloom at the same time. The best floral show is staged on the branches of the previous year's growth. When the branches have finished flowering, cut them back to half or two thirds of their length so the plant will produce vigorous new growth during the summer.

Amelanchier alnifolia **Nutt.**   **Rosaceae**
Serviceberry, shadbush   **Rose Family**

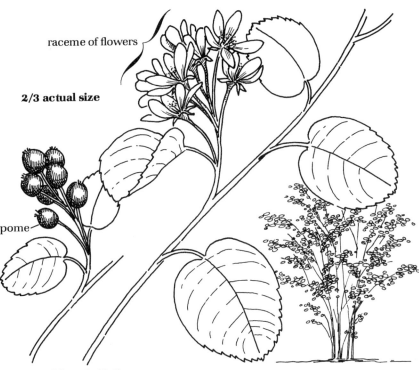

Amelanchier alnifolia
Propagation: Cuttings from August to September, or seeds.
Height: 1.5 to 5 m.
Leaves: Alternate, simple, deciduous. Blades oval to oblong, 2 to 4 cm long, coarsely toothed above the middle.
Flowers: White, 10 to 20 mm long, 3 to 20 flowers in short racemes. Corolla 5 petals, more or less erect. Stamens 12 to 20. Ovary almost completely inferior, 4- or 5-celled.
Bloom: April to July.
Fruit: Pome, dark red to purple, covered with a whitish bloom, 10- to 14-mm diameter, several-seeded.
Range: Southern Alaska to California, from coast to midwestern states.

    Serviceberry is one of the most conspicuous native shrubs when it is in bloom, especially in the dry canyons east of the Cascade Mountains. Its narrow-petaled, white flowers are showy and its thin, bright green leaves have a distinctive oval shape and alternate on reddish brown, young branches, which mature to gray. Birds and mammals are fond of the berries, and the shrub is one of the most valuable and nutritious browse plants of the region.

    The early inhabitants of the eastern states gave the *Amelanchier* group the common name "shadbush" because, at flowering time, the shad arrived from the ocean to ascend the tidal rivers. In the West, it acquired the name "serviceberry" from the pioneers who found the edible, applelike fruits delicious in puddings, jams, muffins, pies, wines, and ciders. They also preserved the fruits in dried form and ate them like raisins. Serviceberry was popular, too, with the Indians, who used it to make pemmican (dried venison or buffalo meat). A word of caution to today's berry hunters, however—the fruit is often wormy.

    Amelanchier is from a French name for a European species. *Alnifolia* describes the shrub's alderlike foliage.

    Beautiful white flowers, edible fruit, and yellow fall foliage make serviceberry a worthy candidate for the home landscape. It is tolerant of poor soil and moisture conditions and survives in neglected areas of the garden. Early in the growing season, kind treatment and ample moisture encourage the plant to grow rapidly. Train it as a shrub or as a small tree, and place it against a dark background to emphasize its leafless winter form.

Holodiscus discolor **(Pursh) Maxim.** **Rosaceae**

Ocean spray, Indian arrowwood, rock spirea **Rose Family**

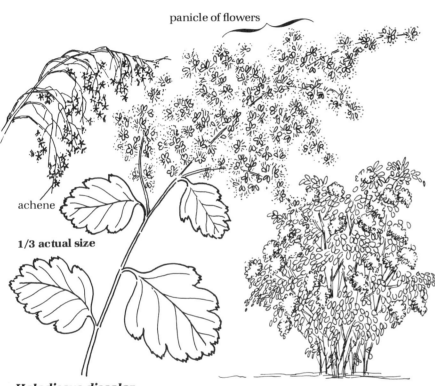

Holodiscus discolor

Propagation: Cuttings from August to September, seeds, or layering.
Height: 1 to 5 m.
Leaves: Alternate, simple, deciduous. Blades ovate, 3 to 10 cm long, shallowly lobed or coarsely toothed, green and smooth or sparsely hairy above, whitish and hairy beneath.
Flowers: White or cream, 5 mm broad, numerous in showy panicles. Corolla 5 petals. Stamens 20. Ovary superior, bearing 2 pendulous ovules.
Bloom: June to August.
Fruit: Achene, 2 mm long, usually 1-seeded.
Range: British Columbia to southern California, from coast to Rocky Mountains.

As its common name implies, ocean spray is often seen swaying its branches only a few feet above high tide, and is most abundant in coastal regions, within reach of salty air. It has grayish red bark and branches that are slender, arching, and flexible. Indians used the younger, more flexible wood for arrow shafts. The older wood is hard and pioneers made pegs from it to use in constructing their buildings.

Weight from the pyramid-shaped, lacy panicles of white or creamy flowers causes the branches to arch or droop even more than usual in the summer. The flowers wither to a soft brown color and are persistent into fall. Ocean spray grows in a wide variety of environments, showing little preference for soil or moisture conditions.

Holodiscus is from the Greek *holo-* ("whole") and refers to the unlobed disk that holds the floral parts. *Discolor* suggests the change in color of the withering flowers.

Because the shrub is so common in the Northwest, it is often shoved aside by bulldozers in the landscaping process. This is unfortunate because ocean spray is an attractive ornamental, especially as a single specimen underplanted with colorful summer-blooming annuals or perennials. Its graceful branches soften the hard lines of a fence or add a soft contrast to large-leaved, evergreen shrubs. A little pruning each year after flowering keeps the shrub tidy and shapely. It develops its best form and bloom if given a place in well-drained soil and full sun.

Ocean spray is so abundant in some areas that there is no harm in moving a seedling from private or public land if you ask permission from the landowner or proper authority. Dig a root ball to avoid damaging the roots and move the plant during its dormant period in late fall or winter.

Osmaronia cerasiformis (T. & G.) Greene
Osoberry, Indian plum, Indian peach

Rosaceae

Rose Family

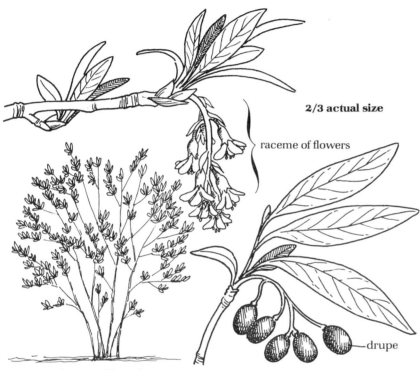

Osmaronia cerasiformis
Propagation: Cuttings from May to September, or seeds.
Height: 1.5 to 5 m.
Leaves: Alternate, simple, deciduous. Blades oblong-lanceolate, 5 to 12 cm long, bright green above, paler beneath.
Flowers: Dioecious. Greenish white, 5 to 6 mm long, smaller on the pistillate flowers, borne in axillary racemes. Staminate and pistillate flowers separate and usually on different plants. Corolla 5 petals. Stamens 15. Pistils 5. Ovary superior, 2-celled.
Bloom: February to April.
Fruit: Drupe, bluish black, 8 to 10 mm long, bitter, 1-seeded.
Range: British Columbia to northern California, from coast to western slopes of Cascade and Sierra Nevada mountains.

Osoberry is an unimposing shrub that produces pendulous racemes of greenish white flowers from late February to April. As one of the earliest of spring-blooming plants, its dainty flowers and bright green leaves are a refreshing sight along stream banks, roadsides, and open woods. When the fragrant blooms appear, leaf buds begin to swell on the purplish brown branches and expose bright green blades that develop rapidly into lancelike leaves.

A close look at the blossoms reveals that the male (staminate) flower has fifteen stamens in three rows and its blossoms are more spreading and whiter than the female (pistillate) flower. The pistillate flower bears five pistils at the base of the calyx tube and produces the orange fruits that mature to blue black. These fruits resemble small plums and are attractive to many species of birds but taste bitter to man.

Osoberry is the only species in the genus *Osmaronia*, and is named from the Greek word *osme*, meaning "smell," and the generic terminal *-aronia*. *Cerasiformis* means "of cherry form" and probably refers to the leaf shape.

Its early, abundant bloom and graceful branching pattern make osoberry a pleasing addition to the woodland garden. You can easily prune it and train it as a small tree or use it in a background planting. Planting drifts of golden daffodils and multicolored hyacinths or narcissus in the foreground creates a picture of spring freshness.

***Potentilla fruticosa* L.** **Rosaceae**
Shrubby cinquefoil, **Rose Family**
    yellow rose, rock rose

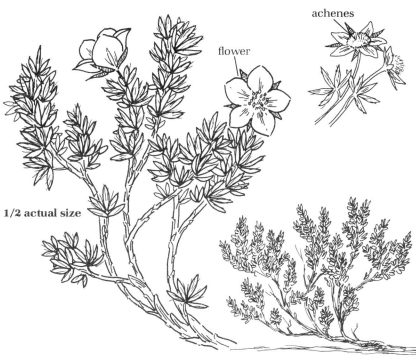

Potentilla fruticosa
Propagation: Cuttings from July to September, or seeds.
Height: 1 to 16 dm.
Leaves: Alternate, pinnately compound with 5 to 7 leaflets, deciduous. Blades oblong, 1 to 2.5 cm long, margins often revolute. Silky hairs give a grayish appearance.
Flowers: Golden yellow, 2 to 3 cm across, on short terminal cymes or single in leaf axils. Corolla 5 petals. Stamens 25 to 30. Numerous pistils borne on an enlarged hypanthium. Ovary superior, 1-celled.
Bloom: June to August.
Fruit: Achene, about 1.8 mm long, egg-shaped, 1-seeded.
Range: Alaska to California; in scattered areas across North America. Europe and Asia.

    Members of the Rose Family have an exceptional ability to adapt to adverse growing conditions; the shrubby cinquefoil is no exception. In its subalpine haunts, it burrows its roots into soil between rocks and spreads many branches over the ground. This prostrate, matlike habit protects the shrub from damage by cold winds and heavy snows on south and west slopes, where it usually grows. A month after the snow has melted, brilliant yellow, roselike flowers face up toward the sun. Below the rock scree, the earth holds enough moisture to nourish the plant through the dry summer. At lower elevations, shrubby cinquefoil seeks moist locations beside streams or in small ravines, and changes its growth habit to become an erect shrub. Birds and small mammals eat the seeds and foliage.
    Its species name, *fruticosa*, means "shrublike." *Potentilla* is from the Latin *potens*, which means "powerful" and refers to alleged medicinal properties of some species.
    Shrubby cinquefoil adapts well to cultivation and is a showy plant for midsummer bloom in the garden. Its bright yellow flowers and grayish-tinged foliage form an interesting contrast with other gray- or green-leaved companion shrubs.

***Rubus pedatus* Smith**   **Rosaceae**
Trailing raspberry,   **Rose Family**
    five-leaf bramble

Palm-shaped, dark green leaves that perch at the top of long petioles, and rose-shaped, white flowers followed by red, jewellike berries are trailing raspberry's badges of distinction. This miniature ground cover grows equally well in subalpine zones on the coast or in interior areas, but always chooses moist, shady, sheltered locations.

At fairly even intervals along trailing raspberry's stems, leaf stalks grow upward, one to two inches high, and support the terminal leaves. Roots begin to grow at the base of these leaf nodes, and new plants are born. This method of self-propagation (known as stolons or runners) allows the shrub to reach six to eight feet over the ground within a few seasons. As its stems thread their way through the mosses and forest debris, trailing raspberry serves a special purpose in nature's scheme—it holds moisture and gives shelter to the roots of taller shrubs and trees that shade the small plant from overhead.

The juicy, red fruit is responsible for the generic name *Rubus*, which is Latin for "ruby" or "red." *Pedatus* means "footed." The small leaves, spaced precisely along the stems, bring to the imagination a vision of bird feet padding daintily across the forest floor.

Trailing raspberry is easy to grow and is one of the choicest native ground covers for the home garden, particularly if used beneath such evergreen shrubs as huckleberries and rhododendrons. The absence of prickles or thorns, which are inherent in the larger species of the Rose Family, adds to the desirability of growing this tiny shrub in shaded areas of the garden.

One rooted stolon makes rapid progress in sending out trailing stems. Place small pebbles or wire hooks over each stem to hold each one close to the ground surface. Loosen the soil below the leaf node and

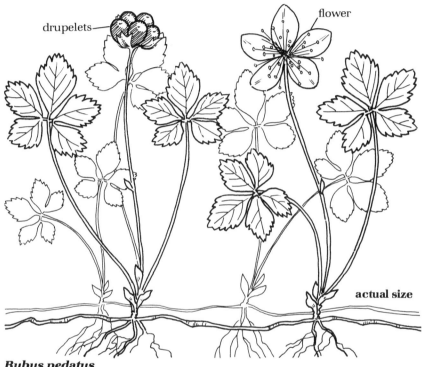

keep it moist so the new roots can penetrate into the ground. To transplant the newly rooted node, just cut the stem between the plants, lift the plant from the soil with a trowel, and place the new plant in its permanent home.

A large patch of trailing raspberry will furnish enough fruits to make a mildly flavored, burgundy-colored jelly, but competition for the fruit is considerable. Wood thrushes, cedar waxwings, western tanagers, pine grosbeaks, and grouse are among the many birds that desire the juicy berries.

Rubus pedatus

Propagation: Seeds or stolons.

Height: Up to 5 cm.

Leaves: Compound, palmate, terminal on a slender petiole; 3 leaflets, 2 of which may be so deeply lobed that they look like 5 complete leaflets; evergreen. Blades oval to somewhat triangular-oval, 1 to 3 cm long, coarsely toothed. A pair of brown, membranous stipules are at the base of the leaf petiole.

Flowers: White, single. Petals oblong, 1.2 to 1.5 cm across with petals and sepals about equal. Flowering stem less than 2.5 cm high. Corolla 5 petals, spreading. Stamens numerous. Ovary superior, 3- to 6-celled.

Bloom: May to July.

Fruit: Drupelet, 1 to 6, red, 4 mm long, fleshy, smooth, juicy, edible.

Range: Alaska to southern Oregon, from coast to western Alberta, western Montana, and northern Idaho.

***Empetrum nigrum* L.**
Crowberry, mossberry, curlewberry

Empetraceae
Crowberry Family

When early spring arrives in the highlands, the thin layer of snow that covers high, windswept, rocky ridges is soon melted by the warm rays of the sun. In this barren, alpine environment, the tough and prostrate stems of crowberry curve upward and lift their mass of shining leaves to the light. In spite of frosty nights and chill winds, tiny brownish purple flowers bloom in small clusters that protrude from the leaf axils and at branch ends.

The crowberry plant produces miniature, apple-shaped fruits in abundance. They ripen by August and are important to the diet of such wildlife as black bears (which forage for the fruits) and tiny, rock-dwelling pikas (which store both the fruit and foliage in their underground dens). When the midwinter snows make other foods scarce, grouse and ptarmigan also eat the shiny, black crowberries, which persist even under snow.

The unique flavor of the fruit was not overlooked by Indians, who ate them fresh, or dried and stored them for later use. Pioneers soon discovered their value in pies, jellies, and sauces. Today, mountain hikers collect the berries and cook a flavorful sauce for hot cakes.

The genus name, *Empetrum*, comes from two ancient Greek words: *en*, meaning "upon," and *petros*, meaning "rock." *Nigrum* refers to the black color of the fruit, which also explains the common name "crowberry."

This hardy shrub is not limited to high mountain ridges. It survives equally well on rocky, exposed sea cliffs or in competition with other plants for light and space in moist, coastal peat bogs.

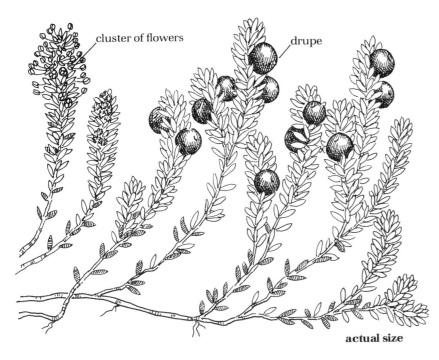

cluster of flowers — drupe — **actual size**

In the garden, crowberry is a slow growing, heatherlike shrub that is desirable as a specimen plant in a rockery or as a ground cover in a small, well-drained, rocky slope. It is also attractive in a dish garden or bonsai planting, where its tiny, evergreen leaves combine in harmony with other plants that have larger foliage. Add basalt or granitic rocks at its base in order to achieve a natural appearing, miniature landscape.

Empetrum nigrum
Propagation: Cuttings from August to October, seeds, or layering.
Height: 1.5 dm.
Leaves: In part alternate, in part whorls of 4, simple; evergreen; crowded along the branches. Blades linear, 4 to 8 mm long, margins revolute, lower surface grooved.
Flowers: Dioecious. Brownish purple, inconspicuous, about 3 mm long, borne in terminal or axillary clusters. Sepals, petals, and stamens mostly in 3s. The perfect flower has 1 pistil. Ovary superior, 6- to 9- celled.
Bloom: May to July.
Fruit: Drupe, black, shiny, 4 to 5 mm long.
Range: Almost circumpolar. Common in Alaska and the Aleutian Islands; extends southward in Cascade Mountains and in scattered peat bogs along the coast to northern California.

Pachistima myrsinites **Celastraceae**
(Pursh) Raf.
Mountain box, Oregon **Staff-Tree Family**
boxwood, goat brush

Mountain box is one of the finest of the native shrubs as it is evergreen, compact of habit, and equally healthy in dense shade or full sun. Its broad range in the Pacific Northwest attests to its adaptability and hardiness in a great variety of climates and elevations. From sea level to the mountains, it takes its place in the forest as a low and spreading shrub, filling spaces under larger shrubs, hemlock, fir, and pine. The delicate beauty and pleasant fragrance of its maroon flowers add to its subtle attractions.

The genus name is from the Greek *pachys*, which means "thick," and *stigma*, which refers to the part of the flower that receives the pollen grains. *Myrsine* comes from the Greek word for "myrrh," meaning "perfume," and refers to the fragrance of the flowers.

Mountain box is a neat, attractive shrub when used in borders, shaped into a low hedge, or planted in irregular drifts. Its small, leathery, glossy leaves are dark green throughout the year and blend in texture and shape with many other garden shrubs and trees. Well-drained, slightly acid soil is its only preference.

Pachistima myrsinites

Propagation: Cuttings from July to September, or seeds.
Height: 2 to 10 dm.
Leaves: Opposite, simple, evergreen. Blades oblong-lanceolate, 1 to 3 cm long, serrate.
Flowers: Maroon, 3 to 4 mm broad, in small axillary clusters. Corolla 4 petals. Stamens 4. Ovary sunken in disk, 2-celled.
Bloom: April to June.
Fruit: Capsule, 3 to 4 mm long.
Range: British Columbia to California, from coast to Rocky Mountains.

***Ceanothus prostratus* Benth.**   **Rhamnaceae**
Mahala mat, squaw carpet   **Buckthorn Family**

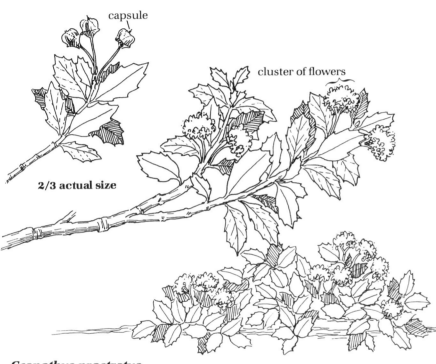

Ceanothus prostratus
Propagation: Cuttings from July to August, seeds, or layering.
Height: 3 to 5 cm.
Leaves: Opposite, simple, evergreen. Blades oblong to obovate, 1 to 2.5 cm long, deeply toothed, hairy on lower surface, rigid.
Flowers: Blue to white, 4 mm broad, from 10 to 30 borne in small clusters that are terminal on short lateral branches. Corolla 5 petals, long-clawed, hooded. Stamens 5. Ovary superior, 3 carpels in the pistil.
Bloom: May to July.
Fruit: Capsule, 6 to 8 mm long, with 3 divergent horns.
Range: Eastern slopes of Cascade Mountains from Yakima County, Washington, to Sierra Nevada Mountains; also southwestern Oregon and northwestern California.

This delightful little ground-hugging plant has airy, blue-to-white flowers and inhabits dry pine forests on the eastern slopes of the Cascade and Sierra Nevada mountains. It also ventures into that paradise of wild plants where northern flora mingles with southern flora in the high elevations of southwestern Oregon.

Its species name describes the matlike habit of this grayish green, evergreen shrub, which spreads three to nine feet across and is only two inches tall. *Ceanothus* is a Greek name for a plant known in the days of the Greek philosopher and scientist Theophrastus. *Mahala* is an Indian word meaning "woman." The reasons for the common names "mahala mat" and "squaw carpet" are unknown, but the names apparently refer to a use of the plant by Indian women.

Mahala mat is a choice ground cover or rockery plant, and is especially lovely when planted under white- or yellow-flowering shrubs that bloom during the same time. Well-drained, loamy-gritty soil and full sun are its main requirements. It must also be in a location that is sheltered from cold winds and frosts. Once established, it grows fairly rapidly.

***Ceanothus velutinus* Dougl.** **Rhamnaceae**
Sticky laurel, mountain balm, **Buckthorn Family**
cinnamon bush, greasewood, tobacco brush

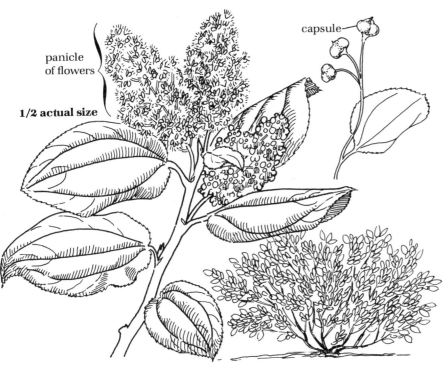

When travelers drop to moderate and lower elevations on the east slopes of the Cascade Mountains, they become well acquainted with the white-flowered, heavy-scented sticky laurel that lines the roadsides. This sticky- and shiny-leaved shrub thrives in semibarren, gravelly slopes where other plants would soon succumb from lack of moisture. At the peak of its bloom, butterflies (especially the pale swallowtail) and bees find the perfume a major attraction, mountain goats browse on its leaves, and birds find the shrub valuable for shelter.

Ceanothus is a Greek name for a plant known in the days of the philosopher and scientist Theophrastus. *Velutinus* means "velvety" and describes the leaf's lower surface.

It is perhaps because sticky laurel is so widespread that people do not think of planting it in their gardens. But in a sunny, sheltered location, it gives year-round pleasure, is well adapted to poor soil and arid conditions, and does not need water in the summer. Its spreading habit makes it useful as a screen for an untidy or neglected corner of the garden, and its sparkling, leathery, evergreen leaves are a fine background for lower growing plants that brighten the landscape with rainbow-colored flowers. In areas where water conservation is essential, sticky laurel more than pays its way—it can go without water for several months and still look green and healthy.

Ceanothus velutinus

Propagation: Cuttings from August to October, or seeds.
Height: 0.5 to 2 m.
Leaves: Alternate, simple, evergreen. Blades ovate to elliptic, 5 to 10 cm long, finely toothed, strongly 3-veined from the base, shiny and sticky above, gray and hairy beneath.
Flowers: White, borne in showy elongated panicles 3 to 6 cm long, spicy fragrance. Corolla 5 petals, long-clawed, hooded. Stamens 5. Ovary superior, 3 carpels in the pistil.
Bloom: June to August.
Fruit: Capsule, 4 to 5 mm long, deeply 3-lobed, the upper part splitting off the base at the calyx line.
Range: British Columbia south to California, from coast to South Dakota and Colorado.

A. Low Oregon grape
   (*Berberis nervosa*)
B. Sweet gale
   (*Myrica gale*)
C. Wax myrtle
   (*Myrica californica*)
D. Tall Oregon grape
   (*Berberis aquifolium*)
E. Hazelnut
   (*Corylus cornuta*)

Plate 1

Plate 2

A. Ocean spray
   (*Holodiscus discolor*)
B. Red currant
   (*Ribes sanguineum*)
C. Mock orange
   (*Philadelphus lewisii*)
D. Serviceberry
   (*Amelanchier alnifolia*)
E. Osoberry
   (*Osmaronia cerasiformis*)

A.

B.

C.

D.

E.

A. Shrubby cinquefoil
   (*Potentilla fruticosa*)
B. Crowberry
   (*Empetrum nigrum*)
C. Mahala mat
   (*Ceanothus prostratus*)
D. Trailing raspberry
   (*Rubus pedatus*)
E. Mountain box
   (*Pachistima myrsinites*)

Plate 3

Plate 4

A. Red osier dogwood
   (Cornus stolonifera)
B. Hairy manzanita
   (Arctostaphylos columbiana)
C. Sticky laurel
   (Ceanothus velutinus)
D. Bog rosemary
   (Andromeda polifolia)
E. Silk-tassel bush
   (Garrya elliptica)

Cornus stolonifera **Michx.**   **Cornaceae**
   var. ***occidentalis*** **(T. & G.)**
   C. L. Hitchc.
Red osier dogwood, creek   **Dogwood Family**
   dogwood

Red osier dogwood is most noticeable during winter when it displays its tangle of bright red branches against a background of stark, snow-covered stream banks and river valleys. In late spring, small, flat-topped cymes bloom and, while the blossoms are not showy individually, the overall effect is magnificent when each branch produces a terminal head of white blossoms.

Many species of songbirds and gamebirds eat the summer-ripening fruits that are unusual in color—waxy white with a tint of turquoise blue. Both twigs and foliage are browsed by moose, elk, deer, and small mammals. Beaver and muskrat use the twigs to repair dams or build dens.

Cornu is a Latin word meaning "horn" or "antler." *Stolonifera* suggests the plant's ability to propagate itself by a natural layering of its lower stems. Its common name "red osier" describes the smooth, red stems that were used in basketry fashioned by Indians.

For a planting intended both to beautify the garden and to attract birds, red osier dogwood is one of the best of the native shrubs. Its thick-growing, free-spreading habit makes it especially useful as a hedge or screen. In its natural environment, it seeks moist, rich soil and prefers the same conditions in the home garden. To control its creeping underground stems, cut off (with a sharp-edged spade) roots that have strayed too far. Also remove branches that touch the ground.

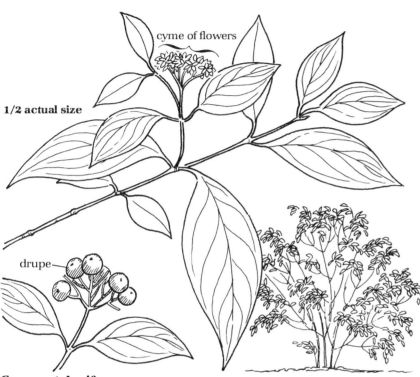

Cornus stolonifera

Propagation: Cuttings from July to September, seeds, layering, or stolons.
Height: 2 to 5 m.
Leaves: Opposite, simple, deciduous. Blades ovate to elliptic, 4 to 12 cm long, conspicuously veined, green above, lighter beneath. Foliage has distinctive 2-way whitish hairs that are flattened to the surface and attached at the middle.
Flowers: White, 2 to 4 mm long, crowded in flat-topped cymes, 3.5 to 6.5 cm broad. Petals 4. Stamens 4. Ovary inferior, 2-celled.
Bloom: May to July.
Fruit: Drupe, white to bluish, 7 to 9 mm long, fleshy, with 2-seeded stone that is somewhat flattened and grooved lengthwise.
Range: Common over much of North America.

***Garrya elliptica* Dougl.**
Silk-tassel bush

Garryaceae
Silk-Tassel Family

The silk-tassel bush is one of the Northwest's most unusual shrubs. When in bloom during the winter months, it displays racemes (sometimes almost a foot long) that resemble little greenish white icicles or silken tassels. The racemes of the staminate flowers are slightly longer than those of the pistillate plant, in which the flowers are replaced by attractive purple berries. Young branches are hairy but become smooth and brownish, and then rough barked.

The genus is named for Nicholas Garry, a personal friend of the famous botanist David Douglas. *Elliptica* refers to the elliptic shape of the leaves. There is only one genus in the family.

This species of silk-tassel bush grows in the mild climate of the often fog-shrouded California and Oregon coastal bluffs. Another species, *Garrya fremontii* Torr., is a plant of chaparral and woodland habitat along the Columbia River in Washington and Oregon and southward to southern California. It differs from *G. elliptica* by having a varying amount of hairiness and yellow green leaves that are not wavy margined, and by developing more compact racemes. Of the two species, *G. elliptica* is the more spectacular plant for the garden.

Pruned and trained against a wall or wooden fence, silk-tassel is a stately shrub, and is valuable as a screen or informal hedge because of its leafy habit. Summer pruning when the plant is young forces it to make vigorous, bushy growth from the base; foliage will then be tidy and decorative throughout the rest of the year.

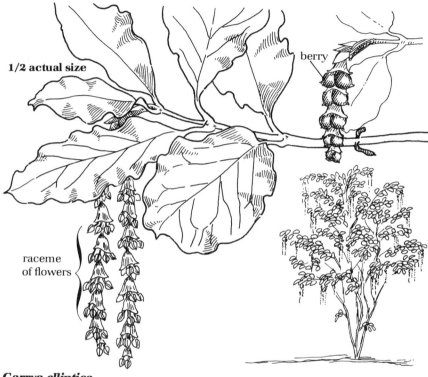

Silk-tassel's beauty reaches a peak in midwinter when catkinlike racemes of flowers hang from almost every branch like belated Christmas tree decorations. During winter, flowering branches may be cut for decoration without impairing the beauty of the plant's form. For the female plants to produce the grapelike clusters of purple fruit that follow the flowers, both male and female plants must be planted in the garden. Silk-tassel also needs the warmth and protection of a sheltered wall facing south or west, acid soil, full sun, and good drainage.

Garrya elliptica

Propagation: Cuttings from July to August.
Height: 2 to 3 m.
Leaves: Opposite, simple, evergreen. Blades oval, 5 to 8 cm long, undulate margined, dark green and smooth on upper surface, gray and woolly beneath.
Flowers: Greenish white, apetalous, borne in pendent catkinlike racemes. Staminate racemes usually several per fascicle, 8 to 14 cm long. Pistillate racemes stout and crowded, 5 to 10 cm long. Bracts are silky. Staminate flowers have 4 elongate, bractlike sepals and 4 alternate stamens. Pistillate flowers have 1 pistil. Ovary inferior, 1-celled, with 2 pendulous ovules.
Bloom: January to April.
Fruit: Berry, purple, 6 to 10 mm thick.
Range: Coastal in Oregon and California.

***Andromeda polifolia* L.**
Bog rosemary

Ericaceae
Heath Family

Bog rosemary is a dainty, evergreen shrub that prefers the acid soil of sphagnum bogs, which are common in coastal and boreal forests and in wet tundra. New plants start by underground runners and grow into a tangled, miniature thicket at the bases of taller shrubs that share the same moist habitat.

Like many other members of the Heath Family, the bark is reddish brown. Narrow leaves that are dark green above and silvery beneath form a background for small, urn-shaped flowers, which hang in an umbel at the end of each branch. Although the plant contains a *strong poison* called andromedotoxin, it is unlikely that humans or wildlife would eat the spicy-scented but bitter-tasting leaves.

The botanist Linnaeus observed that this lovely little shrub is often perched on a mossy mound in a swamp, and related this situation to the predicament of Andromeda (the beautiful daughter of Cepheus and Cassiopea in Greek mythology), who was chained to a rock in the sea. The species name is from the Latin *polio* ("to whiten") and *folium* ("leaf"), and refers to the whitish undersurface of the leaves. Its common name reflects the resemblance of the leaves to those of a fragrant European shrub of the Mint Family that is also known by the common name "rosemary," and is used in perfume and cooking.

Bog rosemary is valued as a garden ornamental. It is a charming plant when grown as a specimen or in combination with other native

Bog Rosemary

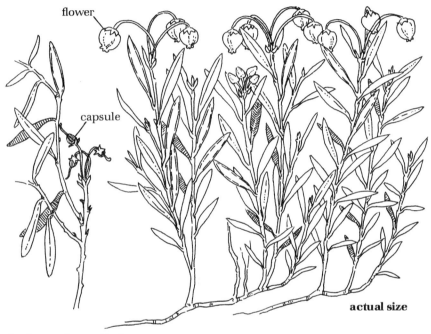

actual size

plants of bog-loving habit, although genuine bog conditions are not essential for its cultivation. It grows easily in acid soil in a moist, cool location. In winter, it adds color to the garden when the leaves become purplish bronze.

Andromeda polifolia

Propagation: Cuttings from June to August, seeds, or layering.
Height: 1 to 8 dm.
Leaves: Alternate, simple, evergreen. Blades narrowly elliptic to linear, 1.5 to 4 cm long; margins revolute; upper surface dark green, deeply veined; lower surface whitish.
Flowers: White to pink, urn-shaped, 5 to 8 mm long. Corolla 5-lobed. Stamens 10. Ovary superior, 5-celled.
Bloom: May to August.
Fruit: Capsule, 4 to 6 mm broad, many-seeded.
Range: Circumpolar. In North America from Alaska to Labrador, south to Washington and Idaho.

Arctostaphylos columbiana **Ericaceae**
Piper **Heath Family**
Hairy manzanita,
 Columbia manzanita

In its native haunts, hairy manzanita prefers dry, rocky environments where the soil is slightly acid. If moisture is sparse, the plants are few and far between and each one grows to its fullest beauty, freely extending its orange brown, angled branches. In summer, the shrub becomes a magnificent sight when its white-to-pink panicles of flowers almost hide the grayish green foliage.

Contrary to its seemingly dry region characteristics, hairy manzanita also does well in the lush, green landscape found from the west slopes of the Cascade Mountains to the coast. In these areas where it receives abundant moisture (especially during winter and early spring), it grows into a thick, tangled, impenetrable mass and covers hundreds of acres.

Manzanita is a Spanish name meaning "small apples" and refers to the small brown fruits that ripen in late summer. The genus name is from the Greek *arktos* ("bear") and *staphyle* ("bunch of grapes") and indicates that bears often feed on the fruits. *Columbiana* refers to its location in western North America.

Grouse, jays, sparrows, chipmunks, and ground squirrels eat the fruits as soon as they ripen; songbirds and small mammals hide and shelter themselves in the dense foliage during all seasons. In some areas, browsing deer keep the shrubs low and extremely compact.

Under proper conditions, hairy manzanita is a splendid ornamental shrub. To show its sculptured form to best advantage, plant it in a rocky outcrop with mahala mat (*Ceanothus prostratus*) or a similar native

Hairy Manzanita

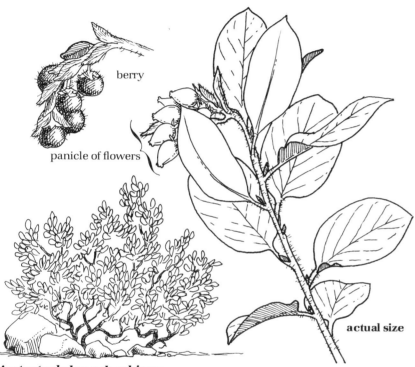

ground cover at its base. On a steep, dry, rocky bank, a large drift of hairy manzanita combined with low growing, grayish-tinged plants creates a striking effect and is attractive all year. Once established, it is easy to grow, with its greatest needs being full sun and loose, gritty, well-drained soil. Moisture in spring and early summer encourages normal growth and healthy foliage.

Arctostaphylos columbiana

Propagation: Cuttings from August to October, seeds, or layering.
Height: 1 to 2 m.
Leaves: Alternate, simple, evergreen. Blades ovate to elliptic, 2 to 5 cm long, finely grayish-hairy, especially beneath.
Flowers: White to pink, urn-shaped, 6 to 7 mm long, in short terminal panicles. Corolla 5 petals, almost united with short, spreading lobes. Stamens 10. Ovary superior, 5-celled.
Bloom: May to July.
Fruit: Berry, orange brown, 6 to 8 mm broad, with 5 stony, 1-seeded nutlets.
Range: Southern British Columbia to California, in coastal regions and on west slopes of Cascade Mountains.

Arctostaphylos uva-ursi (L.) Spreng.
Kinnikinnick, bearberry, sandberry

Ericaceae

Heath Family

Kinnikinnick is an evergreen, prostrate, trailing shrub that roots as it creeps and sends out trailing branches twelve to fifteen feet long. Because it can thrive in poor, dry, gritty soil, dense mats of mahogany-colored branches (often several yards in diameter) check erosion on road cuts, creep over barren rock slopes, or form a compact ground cover under pines, larches, aspens, maples, and madronas. Its reddish brown bark peels from the stems in large flakes, a characteristic that kinnikinnick has in common with related species of *Arctostaphylos* and the Pacific madrone (*Arbutus menziesii*), which share the same habitat.

In late spring, tight racemes of white or pink-tinged blossoms nod from the ends of branches and are succeeded by brilliant red berries that furnish food for grouse, band-tailed pigeons, and bears. Mule deer browse on the twigs and leaves.

The generic name, which is derived from Greek, and the Latin specific name, *uva-ursi*, have the same meaning: "bear" and "grape." *Kinnikinnick* is an Indian word for a smoking mixture, and refers to powdered, dried leaves that Indians substituted for or mixed with tobacco. They also picked, dried, and stored the mealy berries for winter food. There is enough tannin in the leaves for the shrub to be valuable, in some European countries, for tanning leather.

When propagated by cuttings, kinnikinnick usually requires one or two years before it grows an adequate root system and can be placed in its permanent home in the garden. It can also be propagated by seeds, which are removed from the pulp and sown as soon as they ripen. It then may take two years for the seeds to germinate and another two or three years for the seedlings to mature enough to bloom.

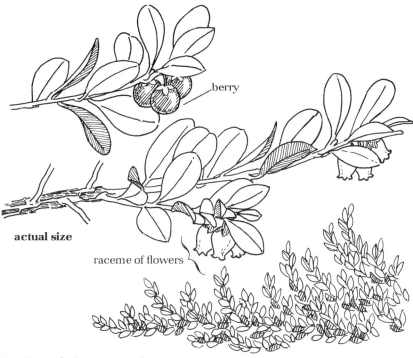

Arctostaphylos uva-ursi

Propagation: Cuttings from August to November, seeds, or layering.
Height: 5 to 15 cm.
Leaves: Alternate, simple, evergreen. Blades oblong to obovate, 1.5 to 3 cm long, smooth to finely hairy, especially on margins and midrib. Leaves somewhat crowded toward ends of branches.
Flowers: White to pink, urn-shaped, about 5 mm long, borne in terminal, few-flowered racemes, slightly fragrant. Corolla 5-lobed. Ovary superior, 4- to 10-celled.
Bloom: April to June.
Fruit: Berry, bright red, 7 to 10 mm broad, seedy, persistent in winter.
Range: Wide distribution along coast from Alaska to California and eastward (especially in the mountains) to the Atlantic coast. Northern Europe and Asia.

It is also difficult to dig up and successfully transplant large, established plants, but you can easily start kinnikinnick by layering. Fine, hairy roots develop wherever a young, trailing branch rests on the soil. Place a few inches of loam over this portion of the stem and keep it moist. Roots will grow and form a new plant. Cut the stem from the parent plant and dig a root ball in order to avoid disturbing the soil around the fragile roots when it is transplanted. Unless the parent plant is easily accessible, layering is, of course, not practical. Instead, you can obtain the plant from a nursery, plant it in the garden, and start layers from it (see "Nurseries and Public Collections").

Once established, kinnikinnick carpets large areas and has few rivals as an evergreen ground cover for steep banks and rockeries. The small, leathery leaves also form a pleasing contrast, in the filtered light, under tall conifers and large, broad-leaved shrubs. For rapid growth, kinnikinnick requires moisture and perfect drainage; the best bloom is encouraged by exposure to full sun.

Cassiope mertensiana **Ericaceae**
   (Bong.) D. Don
White heath, white mountain **Heath Family**
   heather, moss heather

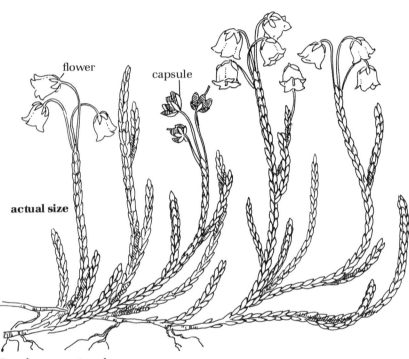

Cassiope mertensiana
Propagation: Cuttings from August to September, seeds, or layering.
Height: 5 to 30 cm.
Leaves: Opposite, simple, evergreen, overlapped in 4-ranked rows. Blades ovate-lanceolate, 2 to 5 mm long, rounded on the back, grooved only at the extreme base.
Flowers: White, bell-shaped, 5 to 8 mm long, axillary, usually several near the branch tips. Corolla 4 or 5 petals, almost united, lobes recurved. Stamens 10. Ovary superior, 5-celled.
Bloom: July to August.
Fruit: Capsule, 3 mm broad, many-seeded.
Range: Alaska to California; from coast to Canadian Rockies, Montana, and Nevada.

Flowers of white heath stand out as sparkling, crisp, white bells against bright green leaves. This hardy, montane shrub (which usually grows slightly below the timberline) favors stony slopes and meadows that are traversed by mountain rivulets. There its moisture-loving roots receive a plentiful supply of water from melting snow. Growth is slow in these high altitudes because of the short summer season; it takes many years for the numerous, creeping, shrubby stems to form a broad mat that is several feet across and up to one foot tall. The small, scalelike leaves overlap and press closely to the wood as they line up in four ridges along the length of the branch. On the lower stems, the leaves may turn brown but remain indefinitely.

The genus is derived from Greek mythology and refers to Cassiopea, who was the wife of Cepheus, king of the Ethiopians. The species is named for F. C. Mertens (1764-1831), a German botanist.

White heath adapts more readily to lower elevations than does rose heath (*Phyllodoce empetriformis*), which resembles white heath and grows in the same high elevation habitat. White heath becomes a desirable rock garden specimen when planted in well-drained, peaty soil, with exposure to full sun and continuous moisture.

Cladothamnus pyrolaeflorus Bong.
Copper bush

Ericaceae

Heath Family

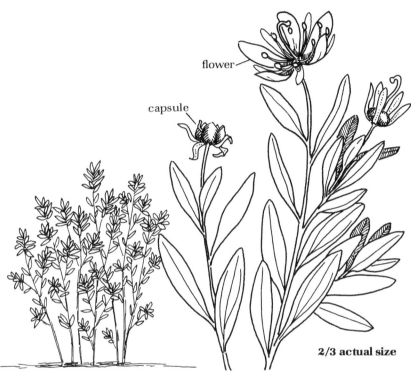

Pyrolaeflorus means "pyrola-flowered" and, indeed, the unique copper-colored flower of copper bush displays the exceptionally long, curved pistil and spreading petals that are characteristic of the genus *Pyrola*. *Cladothamnus* is derived from the Greek *klados*, meaning "sprout" or "slip," and *thamnos*, meaning "bush."

A rather stiff shrub, copper bush has numerous branches that bear smooth, thin, pale green leaves. Solitary flowers with jewellike center parts are borne at the ends of branchlets. Moist, subalpine forests and cool, shaded stream banks that are still edged with melting snow in late spring are its favorite habitats.

Copper bush is not often seen in gardens—such an attractive and unusual shrub deserves more recognition. To keep it healthy, give it growing conditions similar to its natural environment: plenty of peaty soil, moisture, and partial shade.

Cladothamnus pyrolaeflorus

Propagation: Cuttings from July to September, or seeds.
Height: 0.5 to 2 m.
Leaves: Alternate, simple, deciduous. Blades oblong oblanceolate, 2 to 5 cm long, smooth.
Flowers: Copper or salmon color, single, terminal. Corolla 5 petals, 10 to 15 mm long, spreading. Stamens 10. Ovary superior, 5-celled.
Bloom: June to July.
Fruit: Capsule, 5 to 7 mm broad, many-seeded.
Range: Alaska to northwest Oregon, west of Cascade Mountains.

***Gaultheria ovatifolia* Gray** **Ericaceae**
Slender wintergreen, Oregon **Heath Family**
wintergreen, bush wintergreen, western teaberry

Slender wintergreen is a miniature edition of salal (*Gaultheria shallon*), but is restrained in its growth and lacks the larger plant's invasive qualities. A small and spreading shrub, wintergreen is a hardy ground cover and is attracted to a wide range of habitats. Its bright green leaves on slender stems push above heavy carpets of needles in open ponderosa pine forests, form loose mats above the green mosses of high elevation bogs, or appear in sparse quantity on rocky, subalpine slopes.

Dainty, white flowers emerge singly from the leaf axils and are almost hidden underneath the waxy, green leaves. Birds are attracted to the bright red berries, which ripen in late summer and are unique in form—grooved into segments and covered with fine hairs.

The genus name honors Dr. Jean Gaultier (1708-1756), a physician and botanist of Quebec. *Ovatifolia* refers to the oval shape of the leaves.

Of the four *Gaultheria* species native to the Northwest, slender wintergreen is the best choice for a garden ornamental. Success is ensured if this charming shrublet is given shade and moist, well-drained, acid soil in a small woodland garden.

Other native miniature gaultherias are creeping snowberry (*G. hispidula*) and alpine wintergreen (*G. humifusa*). Both species have trailing stems and barely reach three inches in height. Creeping snowberry produces a clear, white fruit and grows mostly in sphagnum bogs or deep coniferous woods from Labrador west to British Columbia and

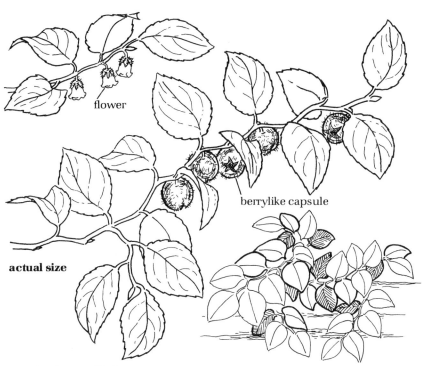

south into northern Idaho and Washington. On the other hand, moist alpine to subalpine habitats are attractive to red-fruiting alpine wintergreen. Its range is from British Columbia south to northern California and east to the Rocky Mountains.

Gaultheria ovatifolia

Propagation: Cuttings from August to September, seeds, or layering.
Height: Up to 3 dm.
Leaves: Alternate, simple, evergreen. Blades ovate, 1.5 to 4 cm long, usually serrate.
Flowers: White, urn-shaped, 3.5 to 5 mm long, solitary, and axillary. Corolla 5-lobed. Stamens 10. Ovary superior, 5-celled.
Bloom: June to August.
Fruit: Capsule, bright red, 6 to 8 mm broad, berrylike, many-seeded.
Range: British Columbia to northern California, from coast to Idaho.

***Gaultheria shallon* Pursh**
Salal

Ericaceae
Heath Family

This species of *Gaultheria* is so common that it may seem undesirable, but its beauty and hardy characteristics qualify it as one of the choice native shrubs of the Northwest. It is a tough, flexible plant that can withstand strong coastal winds, heavy snows, poor soil, and little moisture. Its underground runners scramble through fir and hemlock stands, up mountain ravines, and over rocky sea cliffs, leaving "wall-to-wall" carpeting behind.

Salal is highly variable under different environmental conditions. In dry soil and full sun, it becomes a bronze-leaved, low growing ground cover; in shady situations, it develops dark green foliage. Rich soil encourages the plant to grow one to three feet tall; in moisture-laden air along the Pacific Ocean, it sometimes reaches exceptional heights of up to ten feet.

From late spring to early summer, long racemes of dainty, urn-shaped, white-to-pink flowers arch outward from the mass of glossy leaves. By midsummer, purplish black berries become a source of food that is relished by grouse and band-tailed pigeons. Bears gorge themselves on the seedy fruits, and black-tailed deer and Roosevelt elk consume fruit along with the foliage.

The large, juicy salal berries were an important staple in the diet of the coast Indians and pioneers, and are still used today because they are easily picked and make a delicious jelly (with lemon juice usually added for tartness). As its beautiful, durable foliage complements all colors and textures of flowers, salal is a favored greenery of flower arrangers and florists.

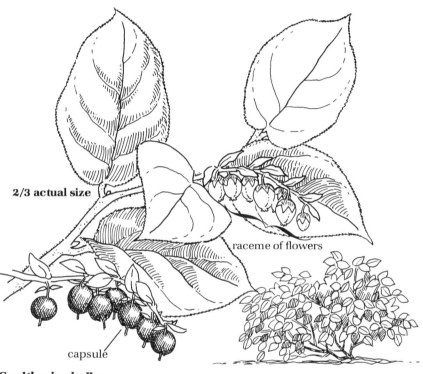

The plant was named in honor of Dr. Jean Gaultier (1708-1756), a physician and botanist of Quebec. *Shallon* is latinized from salal, which is the plant's Indian name.

In cultivation, salal is *not* a plant for the small, urban lot. It is a fast growing, spreading cover and is best used on a steep bank or as a ground cover where it can suffocate weeds and grow with trees and shrubs of equal vigor.

Gaultheria shallon

Propagation: Cuttings from August to October, seeds, layering, or stolons.
Height: 1 to 12 dm.
Leaves: Alternate, simple, evergreen. Blades ovate or oblong, 5 to 9 cm long, serrate, dark green, glossy above, paler beneath. Leaf buds in the axils are pink as are the small bracts opposite each of the flowers.
Flowers: White or pink, urn-shaped, 7 to 10 mm long, in axillary and terminal racemes. Corolla 5-lobed. Stamens 10. Ovary superior, 5-celled.
Bloom: May to July.
Fruit: Capsule, purple with white bloom, 6 to 10 mm broad, berrylike, many-seeded.
Range: British Columbia to southern California, west of Cascade Mountains.

64 Swamp Laurel

***Kalmia polifolia* Wang.** **Ericaceae**
Swamp laurel, American laurel, **Heath Family**
bog laurel

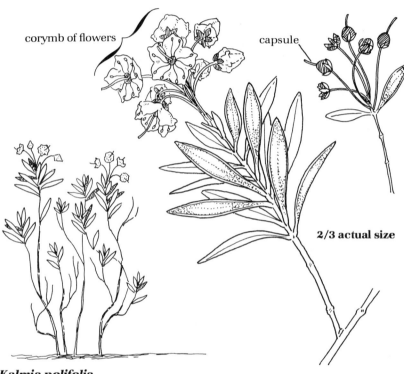

Kalmia polifolia
Propagation: Cuttings in August, seeds, or layering.
Height: 1 to 6 dm.
Leaves: Opposite, simple, evergreen. Blades oblong-lanceolate to narrowly oblong, 1 to 4 cm long, margins revolute, dark green above, finely grayish-hairy beneath.
Flowers: Deep pink to rose, bowl-shaped, 1 to 2 cm broad, in several-flowered corymbs, terminal on shoots. Corolla 5 petals. Stamens 10. Ovary superior, 5-celled.
Bloom: May to September.
Fruit: Capsule, 2 to 3 mm long.
Range: Northern Canada to California, west of Cascade Mountains; widespread in eastern North America.

Elegant buds and flowers make swamp laurel one of the loveliest bog-growing plants. The sculptured, deep pink bud of this evergreen shrub opens into a saucer-shaped flower and reveals ten arched filaments, each with its anther hidden in a slit in the corolla. When the anthers ripen, the slightest movement, induced by wind or a visiting insect, causes them to spring upward and spread their pollen. Swamp laurel has the reputation of being poisonous to livestock and man if eaten, but wildlife seem to be immune to its toxic properties.

Dark green, leathery leaves that have fine, gray hairs beneath are described by the species name, *polifolia*, which comes from the Latin *polio* ("to whiten") and *folium* ("leaf"). The genus was named for Peter Kalm (1715-1779), a student of the botanist Linnaeus.

In the coastal and low elevation swamps, swamp laurel grows two feet tall and is inclined to be somewhat straggly with few leaves on the lower part of its stems. The variety *microphylla* (Hook.) Rehd. is an alpine form that is a miniature, in all its parts, of the larger variety, *K. polifolia*. It is compact in habit and usually does not grow over three or four inches tall. Where the two varieties intermingle, they intergrade.

In cultivation, both varieties adapt to garden conditions and become fine specimen plants. They need peaty soil, plenty of moisture, and partial shade.

A. Salal
   (*Gaultheria shallon*)
B. White heath
   (*Cassiope mertensiana*)
C. Copper bush
   (*Cladothamnus pyrolaeflorus*)
D. Kinnikinnick
   (*Arctostaphylos uva-ursi*)
E. Slender wintergreen
   (*Gaultheria ovatifolia*)

Plate 5

Plate 6

A. Rose heath
   (*Phyllodoce empetriformis*)
B. Labrador tea
   (*Ledum groenlandicum*)
C. Swamp laurel
   (*Kalmia polifolia*)
D. Fool's huckleberry
   (*Menziesia ferruginea*)
E. Trapper's tea
   (*Ledum glandulosum*)

A. Red huckleberry
   (Vaccinium parvifolium)
B. Evergreen huckleberry
   (Vaccinium ovatum)
C. Western azalea
   (Rhododendron occidentale)
D. Western rhododendron
   (Rhododendron macrophyllum)
E. Blue elderberry
   (Sambucus caerulea)

Plate 7

Plate 8

A. Red elderberry
   (*Sambucus racemosa* var. *arborescens*)
B. Squashberry
   (*Viburnum edule*)
C. Black elderberry
   (*Sambucus racemosa* var. *melanocarpa*)
D. Snowberry
   (*Symphoricarpos albus*)
E. Rabbit brush
   (*Chrysothamnus nauseosus*)

Ledum glandulosum **Nutt.** **Ericaceae**
Trapper's tea **Heath Family**

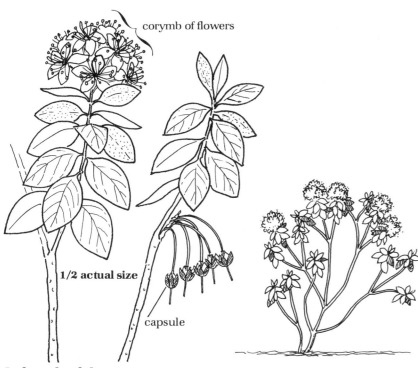

Ledum glandulosum
Propagation: Cuttings from July to September, or seeds.
Height: 0.5 to 1.5 m.
Leaves: Alternate, simple, evergreen, spicy fragrance. Blades oblong, 3.5 to 7 cm long, margins revolute, dark green, whitish and glandular beneath.
Flowers: White, 2 to 5 cm long, mainly in terminal corymbs. Corolla 5 petals, spreading to nearly rotate. Stamens 5 to 12. Ovary superior, 5-celled.
Bloom: June to August.
Fruit: Capsule, 3 to 5 mm long, many-seeded.
Range: British Columbia to California, from coast to Rocky Mountains (mostly east of Cascade Mountains).

Trapper's tea is often mistaken for Labrador tea because both species are similar in habit and size, and both have pungently perfumed leaves and dainty, white flowers that grow in terminal corymbs. Although trapper's tea is usually found in montane habitats, it occasionally grows at low elevations. It prefers to keep its roots in moist soil, and grows at the water's edge where its sprouts creep outward with the sphagnum mosses that gradually fill in glacier-carved basins.

The inflorescence of mainly terminal clusters includes fifteen to thirty white flowers, each nodding from a slender pedicel. At high altitudes, it blooms from June to September; the flowers are succeeded by brown seed capsules that are egg-shaped or almost spherical. This shrub is distinguished from other species of *Ledum* by its dull green, whitish leaves that are dotted with resin underneath. Their thick, leathery texture and slightly rolled margin act to prevent water loss.

Ledum is derived from the Greek *ledon*, meaning "mastic," and *glandulosum* refers to the resinous glands on the leaves and stems. Its common name refers to the fact that early-day trappers used the leaves to make hot tea when they traveled the cold northland, setting and checking their traplines. However, like many other members of the Heath Family, *trapper's tea contains toxic properties and is not recommended for use in a beverage.*

Trapper's tea adapts well to garden cultivation (although seedlings sometimes grow slowly) and like the same soil and moisture conditions that Labrador tea and other bog-loving native plants prefer. A group arrangement of several shrubs of trapper's tea forms an attractive background for pink-flowering bog rosemary (*Andromeda polifolia*).

***Ledum groenlandicum* Oeder**   **Ericaceae**
Labrador tea   **Heath Family**

Labrador tea, named for one of the countries of its range, thrives in acid, wet soil at the edge of peat bogs and swamps where it is associated with swamp laurel (*Kalmia polifolia*) and sweet gale (*Myrica gale*). It has adapted its physical features in order to conserve moisture during droughts. Large scaly buds, twigs covered with brown hairs, and leaves that are densely woolly on the lower surface all serve to slow water evaporation from the shrub. On either cold and dry or hot and dry days, the margins of the leaves tend to recurve to protect the leaves from too much moisture loss. During rainy days, the leaves flatten and expose their surfaces so that the maximum number of cells can absorb moisture into the leaf.

Labrador tea leaves have had a number of uses over the centuries as they contain tannin, gallic acid, resin, wax, and salts. Ancient herbals mention that the leaves were used as a tonic, diaphoretic, and pectoral. Leaves were also strewed among clothes to keep away moths, a practice that is of value even today. During the tea embargo at the time of the American War of Independence, the leaves were used for tea, but because *many members of the Heath Family contain toxic properties*, it may be wiser merely to enjoy the shrub's beauty.

The name is from the Greek *ledon*, meaning "mastic." *Groenlandicum* refers to Greenland, one of the shrub's native habitats.

Labrador tea is an attractive evergreen shrub that has a pleasant spicy odor, which seems to discourage animals from browsing on it, and

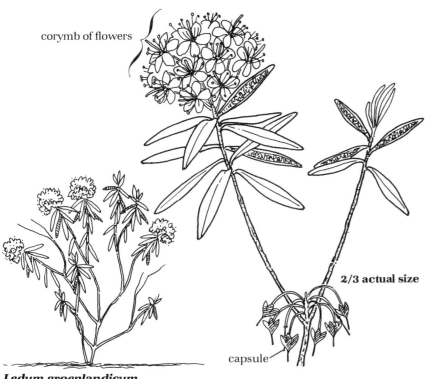

lovely white blossoms, which attract bees. It grows well in an exposed area of the garden where there is wet, acid soil and full sun or partial shade. If you decide to grow it from seeds, keep in mind that the seedlings grow slowly.

Ledum groenlandicum
Propagation: Cuttings from July to September, or seeds.
Height: 0.5 to 1.5 m.
Leaves: Alternate, simple, evergreen, fragrant. Blades linear-elliptic, 2 to 6 cm long, margins revolute, deep green above, rusty and woolly beneath.
Flowers: White, 1 cm broad, in terminal corymbs. Corolla 5 petals, spreading to nearly rotate. Stamens 5 to 10. Ovary superior, 5-celled.
Bloom: May to July.
Fruit: Capsule, 4 to 5 mm long, many-seeded, persistent in winter.
Range: Greenland west to Alaska and south to northwestern Oregon, chiefly along the coast; from Canada south through New England states.

***Menziesia ferruginea* Smith**   **Ericaceae**
Fool's huckleberry, false azalea   **Heath Family**

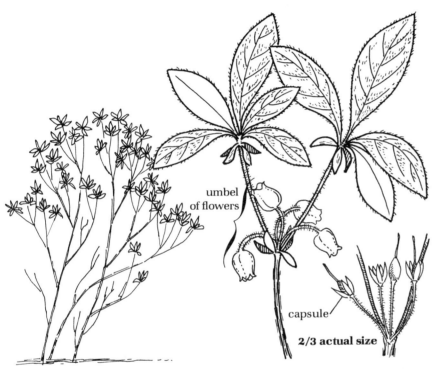

Menziesia ferruginea
Propagation: Cuttings from July to September, seeds, or layering.
Height: 0.5 to 2 m.
Leaves: Alternate, simple, deciduous. Blades ovate-elliptic, 4 to 6 cm long, light green above, paler beneath, somewhat hairy.
Flowers: Yellowish red, urn-shaped, in umbels from terminal buds. Corolla 4-lobed, 6 to 8 mm long. Stamens 8. Ovary superior, 4-celled.
Bloom: May to August.
Fruit: Capsule, 5 to 7 mm long, many-seeded.
Range: British Columbia to central Oregon, from coast to Rocky Mountains.

During the flowering season, fool's huckleberry may be mistaken for the true blueberries and huckleberries, which have flowers and leaves with similar shapes. It is erect in habit, with reddish branches that are often grouped around a larger branch and appear whorled. Light green leaves are somewhat hairy on both surfaces and are spaced alternately on the stems. Clustered at the beginning of the new year's growth are dainty, urn-shaped flowers of a rusty, reddish yellow color. Each flower nods from a slender, hairy pedicel and blooms early, almost at the same time as the leaves develop.

Unlike the delectable fruit-bearing members of the *Vaccinium* species, this huckleberry bears dry, woody, inedible fruits, which is the reason for its common name, *fool's* huckleberry. The genus, *Menziesia*, honors Archibald Menzies (1754-1842), a physician and naturalist who went with the Vancouver Expedition of 1790 and was one of the first botanists to study Pacific Northwest plant life. The species name, *ferruginea*, means "rust-colored" and refers to the rusty glands that cover the branches, leaves, pedicels, and calyx.

Fool's huckleberry grows in moist conifer woods, along mountain stream banks, and at edges of coastal sphagnum bogs where it mingles with its relatives in the Heath Family. As an ornamental, it should be planted in an open woodland situation where its radiant autumn color can be displayed to the best advantage. It adapts favorably to lower elevations and responds to the same cultural treatment that is given to rhododendrons: acid soil, partial shade, good drainage, and ample moisture.

Phyllodoce empetriformis (Smith) D. Don
Rose heath, pink mountain heather

Ericaceae

Heath Family

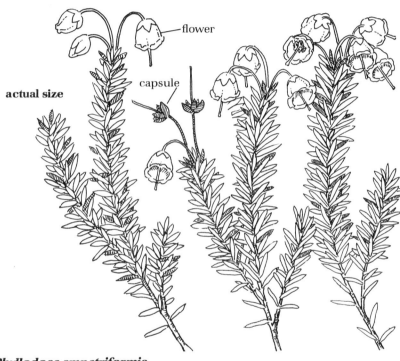

Phyllodoce empetriformis
Propagation: Cuttings from July to September, seeds, or layering.
Height: 1 to 4 dm.
Leaves: Alternate, simple, evergreen. Blades linear, 8 to 16 mm long, margins revolute, deeply grooved beneath.
Flowers: Deep pink to rose, bell-shaped, 7 mm long, single from axils and clustered on stem tips. Corolla 5 petals, almost united, lobes recurved. Stamens 10. Ovary superior, 5-celled.
Bloom: June to August.
Fruit: Capsule, 5 to 6 mm long, many-seeded.
Range: High elevations from Alaska to California, from coast to Idaho and Montana.

Low, brushy mats of rose heath in full summer bloom spread a pink cloud of beauty over alpine hummocks and rocky slopes. But its assignment in Nature's plan is not limited to beautification of the mountains. This evergreen, heatherlike shrub protects the open slopes from wind and snow-melt erosion. It holds moisture and offers shade for the less sturdy perennials and annuals that sprout, grow, and bloom during the short summer season.

The tangled branches are well protected by many crowded, narrow leaves. Where a leaf has dropped, it leaves a raised, peglike scar that resembles the leaf scars on conifers and gives the branches a roughened appearance.

The genus name, *Phyllodoce*, is from the Greek word for sea nymph, a seemingly unsuitable reference for this plant of high elevations. *Empetriformis* describes the leaves, which resemble those of the genus *Empetrum*.

In cultivation, the lovely rose heath grows slowly at lower elevations. Its propagation is perhaps of most interest to the plant collector who rejoices in successfully growing a difficult plant. Besides patient care, it requires a niche in the rock garden that has a gritty mixture of sand and peat, ample moisture, and full sun.

Rhododendron macrophyllum **Ericaceae**
   G. Don
Western rhododendron, **Heath Family**
   California rhododendron

    The magnificent state flower of Washington need not take second place to the brilliant-flowering hybrids that flourish in worldwide gardens. Large, old plants produce an exceptional display of large, pink trusses when in full bloom in May and June. During the prime blooming season, tours can be taken to the Olympic Peninsula and Hood Canal in western Washington State and to Mount Hood in Oregon to observe extensive native stands of western rhododendron.
    The sculpturesque flower buds are deep rose, and gradually swell and open into soft-pink flowers. The splendid trusses contain ten to twenty of the bell-shaped, nodding flowers. Even through the winter, the trusses retain some beauty in the form of brown seed capsules (which expelled their tiny black seeds in the fall).
    This handsome shrub tends to be compact when it grows in the open, but in the shade of fir and hemlock forests, it develops long, straggly branches as it reaches for light, and sometimes grows up to sixteen feet tall. Like other species of its genus, western rhododendron has the ability to conserve moisture by rolling its evergreen leaves backward and inward during a dry summer or a cold, dry winter. The undersides of the large, leathery leaves are covered with colored hairs called "tomentum," another adaptation that keeps moisture from evaporating from the plant in droughts and protects the leaves in freezing weather.
    Both leaves and flowers contain poisonous toxins, so the shrub has limited value as a food source for animals, although mountain beaver do nibble the twigs. The shrub does, however, provide year-round cover for wildlife.

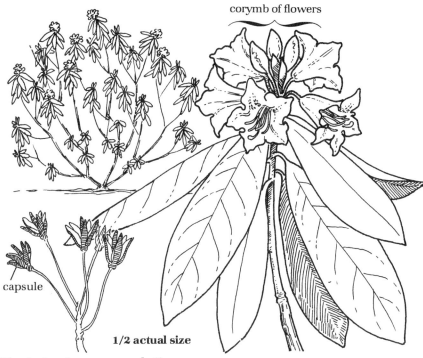

Rhododendron macrophyllum

Propagation: Cuttings from August to October, seeds, or layering.
Height: 1 to 5 m.
Leaves: Alternate, simple, evergreen. Blades elliptic-oblong, 8 to 20 cm long, green above, rusty and densely woolly beneath.
Flowers: Pale pink to deep rose, shallow bell-shaped, 2.5 to 4 cm long, from 10 to 20 flowers in terminal corymbs. Corolla 5 petals, partially united and spreading with wavy-margined lobes, upper lobe dotted with green. Stamens 10. Ovary superior, 5-celled.
Bloom: May to July.
Fruit: Capsule, 1.5 to 2 cm long, many-seeded, persistent in winter.
Range: British Columbia to northern California, west of Cascade Mountains.

The genus name comes from the Greek words *rhodon*, meaning "rose," and *dendron*, meaning "tree." *Macrophyllum* refers to large leaves.

Western rhododendron is a fine addition to the home garden. Grow it as a specimen plant, in mass plantings as a background for smaller species and hybrids, with native ground covers such as kinnikinnick or gaultherias, or use it as a casually scattered shrub in the woodland garden. In cultivation, it needs acid soil, good drainage, plenty of water during the growing season, and partial shade. A mulch of peat moss or coarse bark keeps the roots moist and at an even temperature.

Do not collect this shrub in the wild. If there were unrestricted collecting of this plant, which grows only in limited regions of the Pacific Northwest, it would soon be destroyed in its natural habitat. If grown from seeds, it takes up to seven years to bloom, so not everyone has the time or patience to wait for the first truss. The quickest way to bring western rhododendron to your garden is to buy a two- or three-feet tall, well-branched plant from a nursery and propagate from that plant by cuttings or layering.

Rhododendron occidentale   **Ericaceae**
   (T. & G.) Gray
Western azalea   **Heath Family**

    Western azalea is a highly prized native shrub. Its dark crimson buds open into flowers that are funnel-shaped and have pointed, spreading lobes. Among the plants, there is a wide variation in color—from white to deep pink—and there is almost always a deep yellow blotch on the lower petal. When the warming sun touches the blossoms on a spring day, a pleasant, sweet fragrance is drawn into the air. The perfume attracts insects that perform pollen-distributing missions.
    Western azalea likes moisture and soil that is deep and rich in humus. Seeds take root on stream banks, at the edge of open woods, and in spring-fed meadows and ravines. Mountain beaver nibble the branches, but most animals and birds are attracted to this shrub for the shelter and nesting sites that its dense growth provides.
    Its name is from the Greek word *rhodon*, meaning "rose," and *dendron*, meaning "tree." *Occidentale* refers to its western habitat.
    Western azalea is widely cultivated as a landscape ornamental, and plant propagators often use it in their hybridizing experiments. The shrub is deciduous, but its bright yellowish green leaves offer a pleasing contrast and texture when combined with broad-leaved evergreens or conifers. Its beautiful, fragrant flowers earn a niche for the western azalea in every garden.
    Never collect this plant in the wild—western azalea is rare and grows in its wild state in only limited stands. To propagate western azaleas for your garden, buy a well-branched plant from a nursery and layer it or take cuttings from it. When a new plant develops a good root system, place it

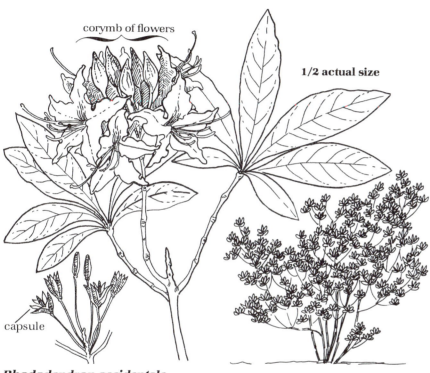

in its permanent home in the garden. *Do not cultivate the soil around the plant;* because the roots grow just beneath the soil's surface, any disturbance can damage the delicate roots. Western azalea needs plenty of water, good drainage, acid soil, and filtered shade. A light bark mulch keeps the roots cool and conserves moisture.

Rhododendron occidentale

Propagation: Cuttings from July to August, or seeds.
Height: 1 to 5 m.
Leaves: Alternate, simple, deciduous. Blades elliptic to oblanceolate, 3 to 9 cm long, thin, yellowish green.
Flowers: White to pink, lower lobe has a deep yellow blotch, 5 to 20 flowers in terminal corymbs. Corolla irregular; tube funnelform, 2 to 3 cm long, about equal to the spreading lobes. Stamens 5. Ovary superior, 5-celled.
Bloom: May to July.
Fruit: Capsule, 16 to 24 mm long.
Range: Sierra Nevada Mountains to southern California, and coastal ranges north into Oregon.

***Vaccinium ovatum* Pursh**
**Evergreen huckleberry,
  shot huckleberry**

**Ericaceae
Heath Family**

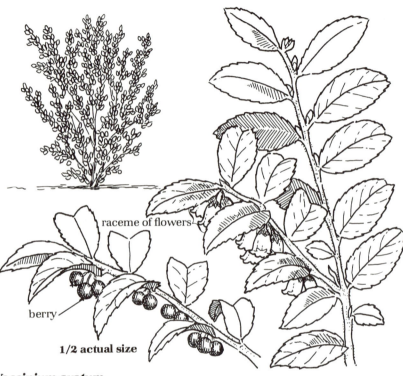

Vaccinium ovatum
Propagation: Cuttings from July to October, seeds, or layering.
Height: 0.5 to 4 m.
Leaves: Alternate, simple, evergreen. Blades ovate to ovate-lanceolate, 2 to 3.5 cm long, serrate, bright green above, paler beneath.
Flowers: Pink, bell-shaped, 6 to 12 mm long, in small axillary racemes of 3 to 10 flowers. Corolla 5 petals almost entirely united, lobes reflexed. Stamens 8 to 10. Ovary inferior, 5-celled.
Bloom: April to August.
Fruit: Berry, black, shiny, 4- to 7-mm diameter.
Range: British Columbia to southern California, west of Cascade Mountains.

To a Pacific northwesterner, the word "huckleberry" recalls visions of juicy pies and oven-fresh muffins. In late August and early September, human hunters of this delectable food invade coastal bogs and mountain slopes. Birds and mammals also find the sweet, juicy fruits irresistible. Being a food source is not the only value of evergreen huckleberry, however. Brush pickers supplement their incomes by picking the dark green, ornamental foliage for the florist trade, and nurserymen propagate it to use in landscaping commercial grounds, city parks, and home gardens.

Evergreen huckleberry flourishes in a variety of habitats that range from coastal lowlands to high elevation meadows. Location determines its form. In full sun with little moisture, it makes dense, compact growth. Under the shade of conifers, the shrub arches its graceful branches toward the light and grows eight to ten feet tall, sometimes becoming spindly.

This species is easy to recognize among other northwest native huckleberries or blueberries. Its thick leaves grow alternately along the twigs in a distinctive flat arrangement that is ladderlike, and the berries are small, shiny, and black. *Vaccinium* is Latin for "blueberry." *Ovatum* refers to the pointed, ovate leaves.

Under all conditions of light, soil, and moisture, evergreen huckleberry is a choice garden shrub because it changes color with the seasons. Its new spring foliage is copper bronze and is followed by numerous bell-shaped, pink flowers, which are succeeded by black berries. Bright green, leathery leaves persist throughout the year. Acid soil and a mulch of leaf mold, peat moss, or bark chips keep this shrub healthy in cultivation, and combining it with rhododendrons and deciduous azaleas creates a pleasing vista of texture and color.

Vaccinium parvifolium Smith **Ericaceae**
Red huckleberry **Heath Family**

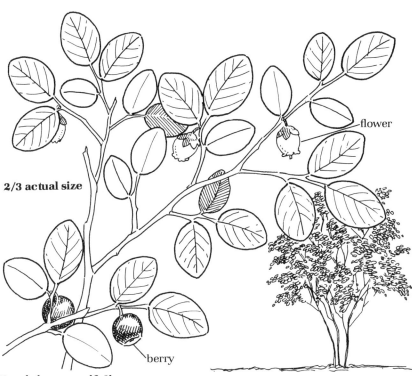

Vaccinium parvifolium
Propagation: Cuttings from July to September, or seeds.
Height: 1 to 4 m.
Leaves: Alternate, simple, deciduous. Blades oval to oblong, 1.2 to 5 cm long, thin, light green above, paler beneath. Vivid pink leaf buds appear in winter.
Flowers: White to pink, tinged yellow, urn-shaped, 4 mm long, solitary in axils. Corolla 5 petals almost entirely united, reflexed. Stamens 8 to 10. Ovary inferior, 5-celled.
Bloom: April to June.
Fruit: Berry, bright red, semitranslucent, 6 to 10 mm broad.
Range: Southeast Alaska to central California, west of Cascade Mountains.

Red huckleberry is distinctive—almost treelike—in its habit of growth. It is easily identified by the smooth, slender, green branches that are strongly angled and ridged and end in a narrow stub.

Although it is commonly associated with evergreen huckleberry (*V. ovatum*), red huckleberry has more definite requirements: low to moderate elevations with moist soil conditions. In logged forest land, it often grows on top of rotting stumps where its seeds are inadvertently planted by grouse and songbirds, which snatch the edible, slightly tart berries as soon as they ripen. Twigs and leaves are a favorite browse of deer, elk, and mountain goats. In locations where these animals are numerous, the shrub is nibbled throughout the year and remains dwarfed. Humans use the red huckleberries to make tasty jellies and delicious pies.

Vaccinium is Latin for "blueberry." *Parvifolium* refers to the plant's small leaves.

Red huckleberry is a graceful specimen shrub for the woodland garden. Single, pinkish yellow, waxy flowers hang on short pedicels, like tiny ornaments spaced along the bright green stems. It increases its desirability as an ornamental as some of the reddish-colored fall leaves persist into winter and are replaced by vivid pink leaf buds. A background of conifers enhances its beauty and gives the shrub the partial shade it likes.

***Sambucus caerulea* Raf.**
**Blue elderberry,
blue-berried elder**

**Caprifoliaceae
Honeysuckle Family**

Most travelers take only a fleeting glance at the myriad of white flowers displayed on a large, much-branched shrub that grows at the edges of woodlands and dry meadows. Little do they realize that blue elderberry is one of the green world's most abundant storehouses of food for wild creatures. Deer and elk browse young twigs and foliage; rabbits and mountain beaver nibble the bark; and squirrels, mice, chipmunks, and many species of birds consume the fruit.

Blue elderberry gained its common name because of the resemblance of its compound leaf arrangement to that of the box elder tree that grows in the river valleys of the southern states. The green leaflets unfold in early spring and are followed by small, white flowers that are clustered in a broad, flat-topped cyme. Although the flowers are beautiful, they emit a rank, pungent odor. The bluish black, round berries also have a white bloom, which makes a mass of them appear to be light blue.

Fertile, moist soils of valley bottoms and sunny, open slopes are favorable to the growing habits of blue elderberry. The shrub grows four to ten feet tall, but in exceptional situations reaches a greater size. Records show it to have attained a height of forty feet and a trunk diameter of two feet. Its range is from sea level to moderate elevations in the mountains where it shares space with firs, pines, maples, alders, madronas, oaks, and sycamores. In arid regions, it is restricted to stream banks and river valleys.

The generic name refers to elderberry's hollow stems, which shepherds used to make whistles. *Caerulea* means "blue," which refers to the color of the berries.

Blue Elderberry

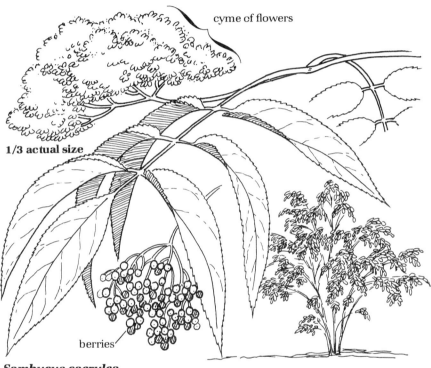

Since pioneer days, blue elderberry fruits, which ripen in September, have been used in pies, jellies, and wines. To clip the berry clusters, use a sharp knife or shears, taking care not to break the brittle branches. *Seeds are somewhat toxic*—be sure to crush and strain the berries before using them for food.

Blue elderberry is desirable in a garden because its berries attract many kinds of birds. It grows in any type of soil, and in either sun or partial shade. Plant it in the background with smaller evergreen shrubs that can hide the bare, unattractive branches that elderberry shows in winter. A mass planting is effective on a slope. Underplant it with kinnikinnick (*Arctostaphylos uva-ursi*), low Oregon grape (*Berberis nervosa*), or mountain box (*Pachistima myrsinites*). To keep the plant dense and shrubby, give it a light pruning during the dormant season.

Sambucus caerulea

Propagation: Cuttings from June to July, or seeds.
Height: 1 to 6 m.
Leaves: Compound with terminal leaflet, leaflets 5 to 9, deciduous. Blades lanceolate to lance-ovate, 5 to 15 cm long, toothed, heavily veined.
Flowers: White or creamy, 4 to 7 mm across; clusters in showy, terminal, flat-topped cymes, 4 to 20 cm broad. Corolla 5 united petals, wheel-shaped. Stamens 5. Ovary inferior, 3- to 5-celled.
Bloom: May to July.
Fruit: Berry, dark blue covered with white bloom, 4- to 6-mm diameter, 3-seeded.
Range: Southern British Columbia to California, from coast to Montana.

***Sambucus racemosa* L. var. *arborescens* (T. & G.) Gray**
Red elderberry, red-berried elder

Caprifoliaceae

Honeysuckle Family

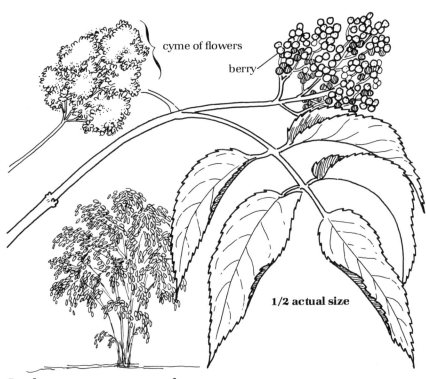

Sambucus racemosa var. arborescens
Propagation: Cuttings from June to July, or seeds.
Height: 1 to 6 m.
Leaves: Compound with a terminal leaflet, leaflets 5 to 7, deciduous. Blades lanceolate to lance-ovate, 4.5 to 17 cm long, toothed, heavily veined, slender.
Flowers: White or creamy, 3 to 6 mm across, clusters in terminal rounded cymes, 6 to 13 cm broad. Corolla 5 united petals, wheel-shaped. Stamens 5. Ovary inferior, 3- to 5-celled.
Bloom: March to July.
Fruit: Berry, red, 5- to 6-mm diameter.
Range: Alaska and Aleutian Islands to California, west of Cascade Mountains.

In the rain forest climate of the north and west sections of the Olympic Peninsula in Washington State, red elderberry reaches its greatest size, forming fifteen- to twenty-foot tall barriers between the roads and the forest. Even in drier regions, red elderberry is of fast growing habit, reaching a height of two to eight feet. It is one of the earliest shrubs to unfold its leaves and, in mild climates, its blossoms begin to open by mid-April. Its magnificent display of white blossoms, succeeded by brilliant red fruits, is an impressive sight.

Red elderberry is one of the most valuable plants for wildlife. Songbirds build their nests in the solid foundations made by the closely spaced branches, bees and butterflies are attracted by the fragrance of the blossoms, and many species of birds eat the fruits that ripen in July. Although the fruits apparently do not cause ill effects to birds or mammals, *the seeds do contain some properties that are toxic to humans.*

Sambucus refers to the hollow stems, which were used by shepherds to make whistles. The botanist Linnaeus gave the plant its species name, *racemosa*, because of red elderberry's large racemes of flowers. *Arborescens* means "treelike."

Used as a background shrub or in a mass planting, red elderberry is attractive from early spring until it loses its leaves in the fall, and is splendidly colorful when the red fruits appear in the summer. Plant medium-sized shrubs and ground covers in the foreground to make elderberry unobtrusive during its rather unsightly dormant season. A light pruning in winter, full sun, moisture, and ample space allow the shrub to develop to its full seasonal beauty.

***Sambucus racemosa* L. var. *melanocarpa* Gray**
Black elderberry, black-berried elder

Caprifoliaceae

Honeysuckle Family

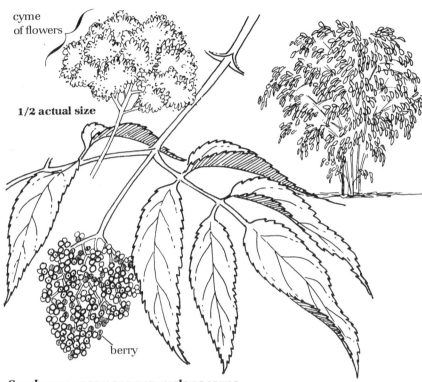

Sambucus racemosa* var. *melanocarpa
Propagation: Cuttings from June to July, or seeds.
Height: 1 to 3 m.
Leaves: Compound with a terminal leaflet, leaflets 5 to 7, deciduous. Blades lanceolate to lance-ovate, 4.5 to 17 cm long, toothed, slender, somewhat hairy beneath (especially when young).
Flowers: White or creamy, 3 to 6 mm across, clusters in showy, terminal, rounded cymes, 6 to 13 cm broad. Corolla 5 united petals, wheel-shaped. Ovary inferior, 3- to 5-celled.
Bloom: March to July.
Fruit: Berry, black, 5- to 6-mm diameter.
Range: East side of Cascade Mountains to Sierra Nevada Mountains in California, east to Rocky Mountains.

Black elderberry is not common in the Northwest, but, at moderate elevations, scattered stands grow where timber has been logged in ponderosa pine country on the east slopes of the Cascade and Blue mountains. It favors a northerly exposure near springs and small reservoirs of late-melting snow water, which provide its roots with moisture late into the hot, dry summers.

Black elderberry resembles both red elderberry (*S. racemosa* var. *arborescens*) and blue elderberry (*S. caerulea*), but black elderberry is a more spreading, lower shrub that grows three to six feet tall. Its large, white inflorescence is rounded and, as the common name implies, the edible berries are black. Foliage is popular browse for mammals, and birds snatch the berries as soon as they are ripe. *The seeds are somewhat toxic, however, to humans;* it is advisable to crush and strain the fruit before using it for food.

The varietal name is from the Greek *melanos* ("black") and *karpos* ("fruit"); *Sambucus* refers to elderberry's hollow stems, which shepherds used for making whistles. The racemes of flowers are described by the species name, *racemosa*.

Because black elderberry is of a lower growing, more compact habit than the blue and red elderberries, it is more attractive in the wild garden. Like the other elderberries, it is not particular about soil or exposure, but does like good drainage. The sturdy, angled branches offer good support and shelter for nests of robins, vireos, warblers, and other songbirds.

Symphoricarpos albus (L.) Blake **Caprifoliaceae**
Snowberry, waxberry **Honeysuckle Family**

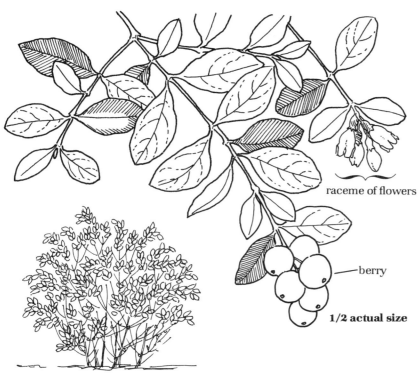

raceme of flowers

berry

1/2 actual size

Symphoricarpos albus
Propagation: Cuttings from July to September, seeds, or suckers.
Height: 0.5 to 1.5 m.
Leaves: Opposite, simple, deciduous. Blades elliptic, 1.5 to 5 cm long, a few irregular teeth, smooth, often slightly hairy beneath.
Flowers: Pink to white, bell-shaped, 5 to 7 mm long, in short and few-flowered racemes at ends of twigs, also in upper axils. Corolla 5 petals, partially united. Stamens 4 to 5. Ovary inferior, 4-celled.
Bloom: May to August.
Fruit: Berry, white, 6 to 15 mm long, 2 nutlets and each contains a seed.
Range: Alaska to Quebec and south in scattered localities throughout the United States.

The generic name of snowberry is derived from a combination of Greek words that refer to the plant's clustered berries: *syn* means "together"; *phorein*, "to bear"; and *karpos*, "fruit." The species name, *albus*, means "white." Certainly, the showy white berries are the main attraction of this common, medium-sized shrub, but bright green, rounded leaves hide dainty pink flowers that are also attractive.

Snowberry is hardy and adapts to a variety of environments—from lowlands to moderate elevations. This tenacious, erect shrub spreads rapidly by suckers and forms thickets, a characteristic that is valuable in stopping soil erosion, particularly on steep banks and in open woodlands that are subject to damage by heavy rainstorms.

The fruits are bitter and humans do not like them, but pheasant and grouse consume them in winter when wild foods become scarce; deer and antelope eat the foliage. The plant's greatest utility to wildlife is the nesting cover and protective shelter that its many branches provide for game birds and small mammals.

The value of snowberry in cultivation is similar to that in the wild: It is most useful as a medium-height ground cover on steep slopes. In the woodland garden, combine it with red huckleberry (*Vaccinium parvifolium*) and trees such as dogwood, fir, and hemlock. Pruning out old wood encourages luxuriant growth and abundant clusters of berries that persist through the winter. Its berried twigs are an interesting addition to floral arrangements of brightly colored fall foliage or conifer greens.

Viburnum edule **(Michx.) Raf.** **Caprifoliaceae**
Squashberry **Honeysuckle Family**

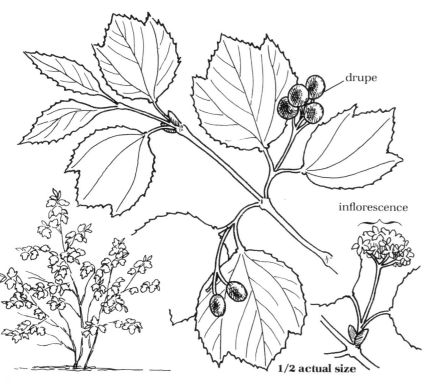

During much of the year, squashberry is inconspicuous, blending its rather straggly branches with other shrubs and trees. Maplelike leaves overshadow the white flowers that cluster in a flat-topped inflorescence. In the fall, however, its dazzling autumn-colored foliage flares in brilliant shades of red and yellow along river bottomlands and on the margins of swamps.

The orange to red berries are popular food for many songbirds, and deer browse the foliage. For humans, the fruit makes a good jelly.

Viburnum is derived from the Latin *vieo*, which means "to tie," and probably refers to the pliability of the branches. *Edule* means "edible."

Under horticultural conditions similar to its native habitat, squashberry develops into a lovely ornamental in the garden. If you enjoy birds around your home, this shrub is a highly desirable species that furnishes food and shelter for your feathered friends. Plant it with conifers and evergreen shrubs that hide its leafless form in winter.

Viburnum edule
Propagation: Cuttings from July to October, or seeds.
Height: 0.5 to 5 m.
Leaves: Opposite, simple, deciduous. Blades obovate, 3 to 10 cm long, shallowly 3-lobed, sharply toothed, palmately veined from the base and bearing a pair of glandular teeth near the junction with the petiole.
Flowers: White, inflorescence 1 to 2.5 cm wide, of 20 to 40 flowers borne on short axillary shoots that each bear a single pair of leaves. Corolla 5 petals. Stamens 5. Ovary inferior, 3-celled.
Bloom: May to July.
Fruit: Drupe, red or orange, 1 to 1.5 cm long, contains large flattened stone.
Range: Alaska to northern Oregon; common throughout northern North America.

Chrysothamnus nauseosus **Compositae**
   (Pall.) Britt.
Rabbit brush **Composite Family**

    This gray-leaved, golden-crowned shrub decorates the arid, high country of its range with massive vistas of fall color. It puts on its best show when other plants have already completed their blooming cycle and have donned drab winter garb.
    Like the familiar sagebrush that grows in the same habitat, rabbit brush rapidly invades poor soils where lands have been overgrazed by sheep or cattle. The roots of seedlings penetrate deep into the porous sandy or rocky soil where there is moisture and protection against the extreme seasonal temperatures that range from above 100 degrees during arid summers to many degrees below freezing during severe winters.
    Two feet is the average height for this hardy shrub, but in especially favorable conditions it may grow to six feet. In barren desert lands it is a subsistence plant for jackrabbits, mule deer, and mountain sheep when other foods are scarce during subzero weather.
    The generic title is a combination of Greek words meaning "golden hued," and properly describes the bright yellow flowers that are balanced at the tips of long, slender, flexible stems. The blossoms emit a sweet, heavy scent that may, at times, be somewhat overwhelming but certainly not nauseating as its specific name indicates.
    In some areas, rabbit brush is so abundant that ranch owners are willing to give permission to remove shrubs from their lands; seeds are, however, the best method of propagation. The shrub is especially desirable in a garden where rainfall is scarce and soils are infertile. A mass planting of this neat and tidy shrub on steep sandy or rocky banks

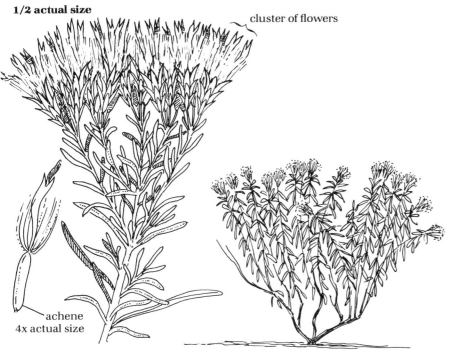

controls erosion, and the bright yellow flowers make an attractive splash of color during autumn. Both twigs and leaves are thickly covered with feltlike hairs that contribute to the shrub's overall light gray-green color. Rabbit brush is a pleasing background for lower growing, brightly colored annuals and perennials that thrive in the same kind of arid environment.

Chrysothamnus nauseosus
Propagation: Seeds.
Height: Up to 2 m.
Leaves: Alternate, entire, deciduous. Blades narrow, 2 to 7 cm long, 1 to 3-nerved, covered with light gray hairs.
Flowers: Yellow, heads in terminal rounded clusters, mostly 5 flowers in each head. Disk corollas 6.5 to 11 mm long. Ovary superior, 1-celled.
Bloom: August to October.
Fruit: Achene, very small.
Range: Southern British Columbia to Saskatchewan, south to California, Texas, and northern Mexico; rarely extends west of Cascade Mountains.

Landscaping Guide

	Bloom Period	Flower Color - White-green	Yellow-orange	Pink-red	Blue-purple	Tan-brown	Fruit Color - White-green	Yellow-orange	Pink-red	Blue-purple	Brown-black	Fruit Edible - Humans	Animals	Habit - Evergreen	Deciduous	Shrub Height - Under 1-1/2 feet	1-1/2 to 5 feet	Over 5 feet	Soil - Very wet	Moderate moisture	Dry	Acid	Light - Sun	Shade
Myricaceae, Sweet Gale Family																								
Myrica californica, wax myrtle	April-May			×					×				×				×	×				×	×	
Myrica gale, sweet gale	April-June			×	×								×		×		×		×	×				
Betulaceae, Birch Family																								
Corylus cornuta, hazelnut	January-March			×				×	×			×			×		×			×			×	
Berberidaceae, Barberry Family																								
Berberis aquifolium, tall Oregon grape	March-May		×							×	×	×	×			×		×	×		×	×	
Berberis nervosa, low Oregon grape	March-June		×							×	×	×	×	×		×	×		×	×		×	×
Grossulariaceae, Gooseberry & Currant Family																								
Ribes sanguineum, red currant	March-June			×						×	×		×		×		×		×	×		×	×
Hydrangeaceae, Hydrangea Family																								
Philadelphus lewisii, mock orange	May-July	×									×		×		×		×		×	×		×	×
Rosaceae, Rose Family																								
Amelanchier alnifolia, serviceberry	April-July	×							×	×		×	×		×		×	×		×	×	×	×
Holodiscus discolor, ocean spray	June-August	×									×		×		×		×	×		×	×	×	×
Osmaronia cerasiformis, osoberry	February-April	×								×	×		×		×		×	×		×		×	×
Potentilla fruticosa, shrubby cinquefoil	June-August		×								×		×	×	×	×			×	×		×	
Rubus pedatus, trailing raspberry	May-July	×							×		×	×	×	×			×			×		×		
Empetraceae, Crowberry Family																								
Empetrum nigrum, crowberry	May-July			×						×	×	×	×	×		×			×			×		
Celastraceae, Staff-Tree Family																								
Pachistima myrsinites, mountain box	April-June			×						×	×			×			×			×	×		×	×
Rhamnaceae, Buckthorn Family																								
Ceanothus prostratus, mahala mat	May-July	×			×					×	×		×	×		×				×	×		×	
Ceanothus velutinus, sticky laurel	June-August	×								×	×		×					×		×	×		×	×
Cornaceae, Dogwood Family																								
Cornus stolonifera, red osier dogwood	May-July	×				×					×		×		×		×		×	×		×		
Garryaceae, Silk-Tassel Family																								
Garrya elliptica, silk-tassel bush	January-April	×							×				×				×		×	×		×	×	

Landscaping Guide 85

		Flower Color					Fruit Color					Fruit Edible			Habit		Shrub Height			Soil			Light	
		White-green	Yellow-orange	Pink-red	Blue-purple	Tan-brown	White-green	Yellow-orange	Pink-red	Blue-purple	Brown-black	Humans	Animals	Evergreen	Deciduous	Under 1-1/2 feet	1-1/2 to 5 feet	Over 5 feet	Very wet	Moderate moisture	Dry	Acid	Sun	Shade
Ericaceae, Heath Family																								
Andromeda polifolia, bog rosemary	May-August			×					×				×	×		×				×		×	×	×
Arctostaphylos columbiana, hairy manzanita	May-July			×			×			×	×			×			×			×		×		
Arctostaphylos uva-ursi, kinnikinnick	April-June	×		×				×			×	×	×	×		×					×	×	×	
Cassiope mertensiana, white heath	July-August	×							×			×	×	×		×				×		×	×	
Cladothamnus pyrolaeflorus, copper bush	June-July			×					×						×		×			×		×	×	
Gaultheria ovatifolia, slender wintergreen	June-August	×						×				×	×	×		×				×		×		×
Gaultheria shallon, salal	May-July	×		×						×	×	×	×	×			×			×		×		×
Kalmia polifolia, swamp laurel	May-September			×					×				×		×	×			×			×	×	×
Ledum glandulosum, trapper's tea	June-August	×							×				×		×	×	×		×	×		×	×	×
Ledum groenlandicum, Labrador tea	May-July	×							×				×		×	×	×		×	×		×	×	×
Menziesia ferruginea, fool's huckleberry	May-August		×	×					×				×		×		×			×		×	×	×
Phyllodoce empetriformis, rose heath	June-August			×					×	×			×		×		×			×		×	×	
Rhododendron macrophyllum, western rhododendron	May-July			×					×				×	×			×			×		×	×	×
Rhododendron occidentale, western azalea	May-July	×		×					×				×		×		×	×		×		×	×	×
Vaccinium ovatum, evergreen huckleberry	April-August			×					×	×	×	×	×			×				×	×	×	×	
Vaccinium parvifolium, red huckleberry	April-June			×			×		×	×		×		×		×				×	×	×	×	×
Caprifoliaceae, Honeysuckle Family																								
Sambucus caerulea, blue elderberry	May-July	×					×			×	×		×		×		×	×		×	×	×		
Sambucus racemosa var. *arborescens*, red elderberry	March-July	×					×		×				×		×		×	×		×		×	×	
Sambucus racemosa var. *melanocarpa*, black elderberry	March-July	×							×	×	×		×		×		×			×		×		
Symphoricarpos albus, snowberry	May-August			×		×							×		×	×	×			×		×		
Viburnum edule, squashberry	May-July	×					×		×			×	×		×		×	×		×		×	×	
Compositae, Composite Family																								
Chrysothamnus nauseosus, rabbit brush	August-October		×						×				×		×		×			×	×	×		

Nurseries and Public Collections

If your local garden centers do not carry native shrubs, the nurseries listed below can supply them.

    Alpenglow Gardens, 13328 King George Highway, Surrey, British Columbia, Canada.

    Arboretum Foundation (annual spring plant sale), University of Washington Arboretum, Washington Park, Seattle, Washington 98195.

    T. E. Bowhan Nursery, 27194 Huey Lane, Eugene, Oregon 97402.

    Forestfarm, 990 Tetherow Road, Williams, Oregon 97544.

    Furney's Nursery, 21215 Pacific Highway South, Des Moines, Washington 98188.

    Green River Nursery, 25041 70th South, Kent, Washington 98031.

    J. L. C. Nursery, 315A Lakeway Drive, Bellingham, Washington 98225.

    Stanley G. Jewett, 23351 Southwest Bosky Dell Lane, West Linn, Oregon 97068.

    MsK Nursery, 20066 15th Avenue Northwest, Seattle, Washington 98177 (specializes in rare plants).

    Northwest Ground Covers and Nursery, 14461 Northeast 190th, Woodinville, Washington 98072.

    Northwest Ornamental Horticultural Society (annual fall plant sale), University of Washington Arboretum, Washington Park, Seattle, Washington 98195.

    Oregon Natives, 1420 North Front Street, Woodburn, Oregon 97071.

    Pro-grow Supply Corporation, 5557 North 124th Street, Butler, Wisconsin 53007 (manufacturer of propagating mats and thermostats).

    San Francisco Garden Center (annual plant sale), 9th Avenue and Lincoln Way, San Francisco, California 94122.

    Schlegel Sunset Nursery, Route 1, Box 161, Banks, Oregon 97106.

    Siskiyou Rare Plant Nursery, 522 Franquette Street, Medford, Oregon 97501.

    Tedrow's Nursery, Route 3, Box 225T, Sherwood, Oregon 97140.

    Theodore Payne Foundation (annual plant sale), 10459 Tuxford Street, Sun Valley, California 91352.

    Valley Nursery, Box 4845, Helena, Montana 59601.

    Viewcrest Nurseries, 9617 Northeast Burton Road, Vancouver, Washington 98662.

The following have public collections of wild shrubs and are good sources of information.

    Charles Huston Shattuck Arboretum, College of Forestry, University of Idaho, Moscow, Idaho 83843.

    Finch Arboretum, West 3404 Woodland Boulevard, Spokane, Washington 99204.

    Hoyt Arboretum, 4000 Southwest Fairview Boulevard, Portland, Oregon 97221.

    Peavy Arboretum, School of Forestry, Oregon State University, Corvallis, Oregon 97331.

    Strybing Arboretum and Botanical Garden, 9th Avenue and Lincoln Way, San Francisco, California 94122.

    University of Washington Arboretum, Washington Park, Seattle, Washington 98195.

Authors' Names Used in Botanical Designations

Most plant books do not explain who the authors are whose names are used in the botanical names of plants. The following list explains those names that are used in this book.

Benth.	George Bentham, 1800-1884. English botanist; longtime president of Linnaean Society.
Blake	Sidney F. Blake, 1892-1959. United States Department of Agriculture, Beltsville, Maryland; student of Compositae and author of *Geographical Index to the Floras of the World*.
Bong.	Heinrich G. Bongard, 1786-1839. Professor of botany, St. Petersburg, Russia; monographer of Brazilian plants.
Britt.	Nathaniel Lord Britton, 1859-1934. Director, New York Botanical Garden.
Cham.	Ludwig A. von Chamisso, 1781-1838. German poet-naturalist; botanist on the ship *Rurik*, which visited Alaska in 1816 and 1817.
D. Don	David Don, 1799-1841. Professor, King's College, London; librarian to the Linnaean Society; brother of George Don.
G. Don	George Don, 1798-1856. Scottish collector for the Horticultural Society in Brazil, Africa, and West Indies.
Dougl.	David Douglas, 1798-1834. Scottish collector and early botanist of northwestern North America.
Gray	Asa Gray, 1810-1888. Professor of Botany, Harvard; author.
Greene	Edward L. Greene, 1843-1915. Professor of botany, California; later Catholic University and Smithsonian Institution.
C. L. Hitchc.	Charles Leo Hitchcock, 1902- . Professor of botany, University of Washington; author of *Vascular Plants of the Pacific Northwest*.
L.	Carolus Linnaeus, 1707-1778. Eminent botanist, professor, Uppsala, Sweden; author of *Species Plantarum*, the foundation of plant nomenclature.
Marsh.	Humphrey Marshall, 1722-1801. Pennsylvania dendrologist.
Maxim.	Carl J. Maximowicz, 1827-1891. German botanist in Russia; director of botanical garden, St. Petersburg, Russia.
Michx.	André Michaux, 1746-1802. French botanist in America.
Nutt.	Thomas Nuttall, 1786-1859. Philadelphia botanical collector and author.
Oeder	Georg C. von Oeder, 1728-1791. Professor of botany, Copenhagen.
Pall.	Peter Simon Pallas, 1741-1811. Noted German student of Siberian flora; eminent zoologist.
Piper	Charles V. Piper, 1867-1926. Agrostologist, United States Department of Agriculture; author of *Flora of Washington*.

Pursh	Frederick Pursh, 1774-1820. Born in Saxony, settled in Philadelphia; author of *Flora Americae Septentrionalis*.
Raf.	Constantine Rafinesque, 1783-1840. Professor, Philadelphia; naturalist.
Smith	James Edward Smith, 1759-1828. England; founder and for forty years president of Linnaean Society.
Spreng.	Kurt P. J. Sprengel, 1766-1833. Professor of medicine and botany, Halle/Saale, Germany.
T. & G.	John Torrey & Asa Gray. John Torrey, 1796-1873. Physician and chemist; author of five major floras. Asa Gray, 1810-1888. Professor of botany, Harvard; author.
Wang.	F. A. J. von Wangenheim, 1747-1800. German forester.

Glossary

Achene Dry, one-seeded fruit that does not split at maturity.
Alternate Leaves that are situated singly at each node.
Annual Plant that completes its life history and dies within a year.
Anther Pollen-bearing part of a stamen.
Apetalous Without petals.
Axil Angle between a leaf and stem.
Axillary Located in or arising from an axil.
Berry Fleshy fruit that contains several or many seeds.
Blade Expanded part of a leaf or petal.
Bract Reduced or modified leaf at the base of a flower or flower cluster.
Bud Undeveloped leafy shoot or an undeveloped flower.
Calyx All the sepals of a flower, collectively.
Capsule Dry compound fruit that splits at maturity.
Carpel Single simple pistil in the female flower, or a single unit of a compound pistil.
Catkin Scaly spike of flowers that usually droops.
Cell Compartment or cavity within which special bodies are produced.
Clawed Having a narrow, clawlike base.
Compound leaf Leaf with two or more distinct leaflets.
Connate United as applied only to like organs.
Cordate Heart-shaped.
Corolla All the petals of a flower, collectively.
Corymb Flat-topped cluster of flowers in which the stalks of the flowers are unequal in length and the outer flowers blossom first.
Cuneate Wedge-shaped, with the narrow end at the point of attachment.
Cutting Part of a branch or root that is cut or broken off the parent plant, then planted so it can grow roots. A plant propagated by this method is identical with the parent plant.
Cyme Flower cluster in which the central flower blossoms first.
Deciduous Falling off after maturity. A deciduous shrub usually loses its leaves in winter or in its dormant season.
Dioecious Producing male and female flowers on separate plants.
Disk Enlargement of the stem around the base of the pistil.
Divergent horns Woody, hornlike protrusions that extend in different directions from a common point.
Drupe Fruit with a fleshy outer part and a stony inner part that encloses the seed.
Drupelet Very small drupe, as in a raspberry or blackberry.
Elliptic Longer than wide (oblong) with equal curvature and rounded ends.
Entire Leaf or leaflet margins or edges that are not interrupted by teeth, lobes, or cuts.
Evergreen Plants that remain green throughout the year.
Fascicle Close cluster or bundle.
Filament Stalk of a stamen.
Funnelform Shaped like a funnel.
Germinate To begin to grow.
Globose More or less spherical.
Habitat Environment in which a plant grows.
Head Close, compact inflorescence in which the outer buds open first.
Hypanthium Floral cup or tube around the ovary.

Inferior   Describes ovary that is below the apparent attachment of the calyx.
Inflorescence   Arrangement of flowers or a flower cluster.
Involucre   Set of bracts that surrounds the base of a flower cluster.
Lanceolate   Longer than wide; widest below the middle and tapering to both ends.
Lateral   At the side.
Layer   Flexible branch that can be brought down to the ground and held in contact with the soil until enough roots are formed on the layer to permit it to be cut from the parent plant.
Layering   Method of propagating plants by layers.
Leaflet   Leaflike part of a compound leaf.
Lenticel   Slightly raised area, composed of loose corky cells, in the bark of a stem or root.
Linear   Long and narrow with parallel sides.
Lobe   Shallow division of a leaf, flower, or other organ.
Margin   Edge.
Midrib   Main vein of a leaf.
Monoecious   Producing male and female flowers on the same plant.
Nerve   Elongated prominent vein of a leaf or other organ.
Node   Place on a stem where a leaf is attached.
Nut   Hard, dry fruit that is larger and thicker than an achene and usually one-seeded.
Nutlet   Small nut that contains one seed.
Oblanceolate   Longer than wide; widest near the top and gradually tapering to the base.
Oblong   Shaped like a rectangle with rounded ends.
Obovate   Widest near the top and narrows abruptly to the base.
Opposite   Leaves that are situated directly across from each other at the same node.
Orbicular   Circular in form.
Oval   Oblong-rounded in shape.
Ovary   Seed-bearing part of the pistil.
Ovate   Broadest near the base and narrows abruptly to the top.
Ovule   Immature seed.
Palmate   Three or more lobes of leaflets, or other organs, arising and spreading from a common point.
Panicle   Branched arrangement of flowers, as in a raceme.
Pedicel   Stalk of a single flower.
Perianth   Sepals and petals, collectively.
Persistent   Remaining attached to the plant after the normal function has been completed.
Petal   Part of the corolla and usually colored.
Petiole   Leaf stalk.
Pinnate   Arranged along the side of an axis, as are the parts of a feather.
Pistil   Female organ of a flower, consisting of an ovary, style, and stigma.
Pistillate flower   Bearing pistils but no stamens.
Pome   Fleshy, applelike fruit that encloses the papery or bony structure that carries the seeds.
Raceme   Flower cluster in which flowers are borne along a stem on individual stalks about equal in length.
Recurved   Curved backward.
Reflexed   Turned sharply backward.
Reniform   Kidney-shaped.

Revolute   Rolled backward.
Rotate   Wheel or saucer-shaped.
Runner   Slender basal branch that roots at the free end, forming a new plant.
Saccate   Sac-shaped.
Samara   Dry, winged fruit, usually one-seeded.
Sepal   Unit of the calyx, generally green.
Serrate   Saw-toothed.
Simple   Unbranched or undivided.
Spike   Dense, elongated inflorescence.
Spinulose   Having small spines.
Stamen   Pollen-bearing organ of a flower, consisting of anther and filament.
Staminate flower   Bearing stamens but no pistil.
Stigma   Pollen-receiving part of the pistil.
Stipules   A pair of appendages at the base of the leaf stalk.
Stolon   Basal branch that forms roots when it comes in contact with the soil.
Stoloniferous shrubs   Shrubs whose branches, after touching ground, root readily.
Style   Stemlike part of the pistil between the stigma and the ovary.
Sucker   Shoot that starts below the ground, from the root or an underground stem.
Suckering shrubs   Shrubs that habitually send up shoots from their roots.
Superior   Describes ovary that is borne above the attachment of the calyx.

Thorn   Woody, stiff, modified stem with a sharp point.
Tomentum   Dense covering of woolly hairs.
Umbel   Flat-topped inflorescence in which the pedicels arise from the same point.
Undulate   Wavy.
Unisexual   Having either stamens or pistils, but not both.
Vein   Vascular bundles of a leaf, or the ribs in a leaf.
Whorl   Circle of plant organs radiating from a common plant.

Further Reading

Brown, George E. *The Pruning of Trees, Shrubs and Conifers.* London: Faber and Faber, 1977. Complete guide to pruning all kinds of plants.

Crockett, James Underwood and Editors of Time-Life Books. *Landscape Gardening.* New York: Time-Life Books, 1971. General introduction to landscape principles.

Gilkey, Helen M. and Dennis, La Rea J. *Handbook of Northwestern Plants.* Corvallis, Oreg.: Oregon State University Bookstores, Inc., 1975. Identifying northwest native plants.

Givens, Harold. *Landscape it Yourself.* New York: Harcourt, Brace, Jovanovich, 1977. Designing and implementing landscape plans for your garden.

Grant, John A. and Grant, Carol L. *Trees and Shrubs for Pacific Northwest Gardens.* Palo Alto, Calif.: Pacific Books, Publishers, 1974. Fundamentals of gardening and garden maintenance; what to grow and how to grow it.

Hammett, K. R. W. *Plant Propagation.* New York: Drake Publishers Inc., 1977. Basics of plant propagating.

Hitchcock, C. Leo; Cronquist, Arthur; Ownbey, Marion; and Thompson, J. W. *Vascular Plants of the Pacific Northwest.* Seattle and London: University of Washington Press, 1977. This technical, five-volume set is the most complete work available for identifying northwest native plants. A condensed version in one volume, *Flora of the Pacific Northwest*, published in 1976, is useful for students in botany.

Lyons, C. P. *Trees, Shrubs and Flowers to Know in Washington.* Toronto, Canada: J. M. Dent & Sons Ltd., 1975. Field guide to knowing native trees and shrubs.

Martin, Alexander C.; Zim, Herbert S.; and Nelson, Arnold L. *American Wildlife and Plants.* New York: Dover Publications Inc., 1961. Use of native plants by birds and mammals in the United States.

Peck, Morton Eaton. *A Manual of the Higher Plants of Oregon.* Portland, Oreg.: Binfords and Mort in cooperation with Oregon State University Press and National Science Foundation, 1961. Identifying shrubs in Oregon.

Porter, C. L. *Taxonomy of Flowering Plants.* San Francisco: W. H. Freeman and Company, 1967. Classification of plants; includes diagrams of floral parts of families.

Schopmeyer, C. S. *Seeds of Woody Plants in the United States* (Agriculture Handbook No. 450). Washington, D.C.: Forest Service, United States Department of Agriculture, 1974. Handling seeds; includes many shrubs from the Pacific Northwest.

Seymour, E. L. D. *The Wise Garden Encyclopedia.* New York: Grosset & Dunlap, 1970. General guide to gardening, soil, and plants.

Smith, James Payne, Jr. *Vascular Plant Families.* Eureka, Calif.: Mad River Press, Inc., 1977. Introduction to the families of vascular plants native to North America and selected families of ornamental or economic importance; includes an excellent illustrated glossary.

Editors of Sunset Magazine and Sunset Books. *Sunset Western Garden Book.* Menlo Park, Calif.: Lane Publishing Co., 1977. Soils, planting mixes, planting, watering, plant protection, tools, and a list of many plants that are suitable for western gardens.

Viereck, Leslie A. and Little, Elbert L., Jr. *Alaska Trees and Shrubs* (Agriculture Handbook No. 410). Washington, D.C.: Forest Service, United States Department of Agriculture, 1972. Botanical descriptions of trees and shrubs that grow in Alaska.

Index

Boldface numerals indicate pages on which illustrations appear.

Abbreviations, 87-88
Amelanchier alnifolia, pl. 2, **38**, 84
American laurel, **64**
Andromeda polifolia, pl. 4, 52-**53**, 85
Arctostaphylos columbiana, pl. 4, 54-**55**, 85
Arctostaphylos uva-ursi, 56-**57**, pl. 5, 85
Arrowwood, Indian, **39**
Azalea, false, **68**
Azalea, western, 72-**73**, pl. 7, 85

Balm, mountain, **48**
Barberry Family, 32-**35**, 84
Bearberry, 56-**57**
Berberidaceae, 32-**35**, 84
Berberis aquifolium, pl. 1, 32-**33**, 84
Berberis nervosa, pl. 1, 34-**35**, 84
Betulaceae, 30-**31**, 84
Birch Family, 30-**31**, 84
Black-berried elder, **79**
Black elderberry, **79**, pl. 8, 85
Blood currant, **36**
Blue-berried elder, 76-**77**
Blue elderberry, 76-**77**, pl. 7, 85
Bog laurel, **64**
Bog rosemary, pl. 4, 52-**53**, 85
Botanical abbreviations, 87-88

Botanical terms, 23-26, 89-91
Bramble, five-leaf, 42-**43**
Buckthorn Family, **47-48**, 84
Bush wintergreen, 60-**61**

California rhododendron, 70-**71**
Caprifoliaceae, 76-**81**, 85
Cassiope mertensiana, **58**, pl. 5, 85
Ceanothus prostratus, pl. 3, **47**, 84
Ceanothus velutinus, pl. 4, **48**, 84
Celastraceae, **46**, 84
Chrysothamnus nauseosus, 82-**83**, pl. 8, 85
Cinnamon bush, **48**
Cinquefoil, shrubby, pl. 3, **41**, 84
Cladothamnus pyrolaeflorus, **59**, pl. 5, 85
Cold frame, 18-**19**
Collecting wild shrubs, 14
Columbia manzanita, 54-**55**
Compositae, 82-**83**, 85
Composite Family, 82-**83**, 85
Copper bush, **59**, pl. 5, 85
Cornaceae, **49**, 84
Cornus stolonifera, pl. 4, **49**, 84
Corylus cornuta, pl. 1, 30-**31**, 84
Creek dogwood, **49**
Crowberry, pl. 3, 44-**45**, 84
Crowberry Family, 44-**45**, 84
Curlewberry, 44-**45**
Currant, blood, **36**

Currant, red, pl. 2, **36**
Currant, red flowering, **36**
Cuttings, 15-**19**, **20**

Dogwood, creek, **49**
Dogwood Family, **49**, 84
Dogwood, red osier, pl. 4, **49**, 84

Elderberry, black, **79**, pl. 8, 85
Elderberry, blue, 76-**77**, pl. 7, 85
Elderberry, red, **78**, 85
Elder, black-berried, **79**
Elder, blue-berried, 76-**77**
Elder, red-berried, **78**
Empetraceae, 44-**45**, 84
Empetrum nigrum, pl. 3, 44-**45**, 84
Ericaceae, 52-**75**, 85
Evergreen huckleberry, **74**, pl. 7, 85

False azalea, **68**
Fertilizer, 20
Filbert, 30-**31**
Five-leaf bramble, 42-**43**
Fool's huckleberry, **68**, pl. 6, 85

Garryaceae, 50-**51**, 84
Garrya elliptica, pl. 4, 50-**51**, 84
Gaultheria ovatifolia, 60-**61**, pl. 5, 85
Gaultheria shallon, 62-**63**, pl. 5, 85

Goat brush, **46**
Gooseberry and Currant Family, **36**, 84
Greasewood, **48**
Grossulariaceae, **36**, 84
Ground layering, **21**-22

Hairy manzanita, pl. 4, 54-**55**, 85
Hazelnut, pl. 1, 30-**31**, 84
Heather, moss, **58**
Heather, pink mountain, **69**
Heather, white mountain, **58**
Heath Family, 52-**75**, 85
Heath, rose, **69**, pl. 6, 85
Heath, white, **58**, pl. 5, 85
Heel cuttings, **16**
Holodiscus discolor, pl. 2, **39**, 84
Honeysuckle Family, 76-**81**, 85
Huckleberry, evergreen, **74**, pl. 7, 85
Huckleberry, fool's, **68**, pl. 6, 85
Huckleberry, red, **75**, pl. 7, 85
Huckleberry, shot, **74**
Hydrangeaceae, **37**, 84
Hydrangea Family, **37**, 84

Identifying plants, **25**-26, 89-91
Indian arrowwood, **39**
Indian peach, **40**
Indian plum, **40**

Kalmia polifolia, **64**, pl. 6, 85
Kinnikinnick, 56-**57**, pl. 5, 85

Labrador tea, 66-**67**, pl. 6, 85
Landscaping, 12-14
Layering, **21**
Laurel, American, **64**
Laurel, bog, **64**
Laurel, sticky, pl. 4, **48**, 84
Laurel, swamp, **64**, pl. 6, 85
Ledum glandulosum, **65**, pl. 6, 85
Ledum groenlandicum, 66-**67**, pl. 6, 85

Mahala mat, pl. 3, **47**, 84
Mahonia, 32-**33**
Mahonia, low, 34-**35**
Manzanita, Columbia, 54-**55**
Manzanita, hairy, pl. 4, 54-**55**, 85
Measurements, 6
Menziesia ferruginea, **68**, pl. 6, 85
Mock orange, pl. 2, **37**, 84
Mossberry, 44-**45**
Moss heather, **58**
Mountain balm, **48**
Mountain box, pl. 3, **46**, 84
Myrica californica, pl. 1, **28**, 84
Myricaceae, **28**-**29**, 84
Myrica gale, pl. 1, **29**, 84
Myrtle, wax, **28**

Nurseries, 86

Ocean spray, pl. 2, **39**, 84
Orange, mock, pl. 2, **37**, 84
Oregon boxwood, **46**
Oregon grape, low, pl. 1, 34-**35**, 84
Oregon grape, tall, pl. 1, 32-**33**, 84
Oregon wintergreen, 60-**61**
Osmaronia cerasiformis, pl. 2, **40**, 84
Osoberry, pl. 2, **40**, 84

Pachistima myrsinites, pl. 3, **46**, 84
Peach, Indian, **40**
Pesticides, 13-14
Philadelphus lewisii, pl. 2, **37**, 84
Phyllodoce empetriformis, **69**, pl. 6, 85
Pink mountain heather, **69**
Plant identification, **25**-26, 89-91
Planting, 19, **20**
Plant names, 23-25, 87-88
Plant nurseries, 86
Plants, public collections of, 86
Plum, Indian, **40**
Potentilla fruticosa, pl. 3, **41**, 84
Potting, **18**
Propagating mat, 17-18
Propagation, 15-**22**

Rabbit brush, 82-**83**, pl. 8, 85

Raspberry, trailing, pl. 3, 42-**43**, 84
Red-berried elder, **78**
Red currant, pl. 2, **36**, 84
Red elderberry, **78**, pl. 8, 85
Red flowering currant, **36**
Red huckleberry, **75**, pl. 7, 85
Red osier dogwood, pl. 4, **49**, 84
Rhamnaceae, **47-48**, 84
Rhododendron, California, 70-**71**
Rhododendron macrophyllum, 70-**71**, pl. 7, 85
Rhododendron occidentale, 72-**73**, pl. 7, 85
Rhododendron, western, 70-**71**, pl. 7, 85
Ribes sanguineum, pl. 2, **36**, 84
Rock rose, **41**
Rock spirea, **39**
Rosaceae, **38-43**, 84
Rose Family, **38-43**, 84
Rose heath, **69**, pl. 6, 85
Rosemary, bog, pl. 4, 52-**53**, 85
Rose, rock, **41**
Rose, yellow, **41**
Rubus pedatus, pl. 3, 42-**43**, 84
Runners, **22**

Salal, 62-**63**, pl. 5, 85
Sambucus caerulea, 76-**77**, pl. 7, 85
Sambucus racemosa var. *arborescens*, **78**, pl. 8, 85
Sambucus racemosa var. *melanocarpa*, **79**, pl. 8, 85
Sandberry, 56-**57**
Seeds, propagating by, **20**-21
Serviceberry, pl. 2, **38**, 84
Shadbush, **38**
Shot huckleberry, **74**
Shrubby cinquefoil, pl. 3, **41**, 84
Silk-tassel bush, pl. 4, 50-**51**, 84
Silk-Tassel Family, 50-**51**, 84
Slender wintergreen, 60-**61**, pl. 5, 85
Snowberry, **80**, pl. 8, 85
Spirea, rock **39**
Squashberry, **81**, pl. 8, 85
Squaw carpet, **47**
Staff-Tree Family, **46**, 84
Sticky laurel, pl. 4, **48**, 84
Stolons, **22**
Suckers, **22**
Swamp laurel, **64**, pl. 6, 85
Sweet gale, pl. 1, **29**, 84
Sweet Gale Family, **28-29**, 84
Symphoricarpos albus, **80**, pl. 8, 85

Teaberry, western, 60-**61**
Tea, Labrador, 66-**67**, pl. 6, 85
Tea, trapper's, **65**, pl. 6, 85
Terms, botanical, 23-26, 89-91
Tobacco brush, **48**
Trailing raspberry, pl. 3, 42-**43**, 84
Trapper's tea, **65**, pl. 6, 85

Vaccinium ovatum, **74**, pl. 7, 85
Vaccinium parvifolium, **75**, pl. 7, 85
Viburnum edule, **81**, pl. 8, 85

Waxberry, **80**
Wax myrtle, pl. 1, **28**, 84
Western azalea, 72-**73**, pl. 7, 85
Western rhododendron, 70-**71**, pl. 7, 85
Western teaberry, 60-**61**
White heath, **58**, pl. 5, 85
White mountain heather, **58**
Wild shrubs, collecting, 14
Wintergreen, bush, 60-**61**
Wintergreen, Oregon, 60-**61**
Wintergreen, slender, 60-**61**, pl. 5, 85
Wounding stems, **16**

Yellow rose, **41**

Other Books from Pacific Search Press

Asparagus: The Sparrowgrass Cookbook by Autumn Stanley
Bone Appétit! Natural Food for Pets by Frances Sheridan Goulart
Butterflies Afield in the Pacific Northwest by William Neill/Douglas Hepburn, photography
The Carrot Cookbook by Ann Saling
Cascade Companion by Susan Schwartz/Bob and Ira Spring, photography
Common Seaweeds of the Pacific Coast by J. Robert Waaland
The Crawfish Cookbook by Norma S. Upson
Cross-Country Downhill and Other Nordic Mountain Skiing Techniques by Steve Barnett
The Dogfish Cookbook by Russ Mohney
Fire and Ice: The Cascade Volcanoes by Stephen L. Harris
The Green Tomato Cookbook by Paula Simmons
Little Mammals of the Pacific Northwest by Ellen B. Kritzman
Living Shores of the Pacific Northwest by Lynwood Smith/Bernard Nist, photography
Make It and Take It: Homemade Gear for Camp and Trail by Russ Mohney
Messages from the Shore by Victor B. Scheffer
Minnie Rose Lovgreen's Recipe for Raising Chickens by Minnie Rose Lovgreen
Rhubarb Renaissance: A Cookbook by Ann Saling
The Salmon Cookbook by Jerry Dennon
Sleek & Savage: North America's Weasel Family by Delphine Haley
Spinning and Weaving with Wool by Paula Simmons
Why Wild Edibles? The Joys of Finding, Fixing, and Tasting by Russ Mohney
Wild Mushroom Recipes by Puget Sound Mycological Society
The Zucchini Cookbook by Paula Simmons